For as long as anyone can remember, we've travelled the world with Alan Whicker. On screen and in print, the familiar voice and eavesdropping style have always unlocked the flavour and texture of people and places. In his brilliant Channel 4 series, and now in this latest book *Whicker's War*, he emerges from behind the camera to talk us through the fear and frenzy of World War II's first great assault landing. Then he goes with Montgomery's Eighth Army as it pursues Kesselring's Wehrmacht up the boot of Italy, from the Sicilian beaches to the Alps.

German prisoners said the Italian war was tougher than Stalingrad. Certainly there was drama and tragedy enough – yet in wartime, fragments of courage and nobility can pass unnoticed. Fortunately Whicker was there to see and remember. In this true adventure story he survives violent death during 660 days of the most desperate and bloody fighting of World War II.

Whicker, battle cameraman and Director of the Army Film Unit, served with a vain Allied General so determined to win public credit for liberating Rome that his disobedience lengthened the war by many months. He filmed the gruesome spectacle of Dictator Benito Mussolini hanging upside down outside a Milan garage alongside his loyal mistress, Clara Petacci. He captured the traitor John Amery, the Lord Haw-Haw of Radio Rome.

Rather to his surprise, Whicker also accepted the surrender of the last stronghold of the dreaded German SS in Italy – the brutal army police force founded by Adolf Hitler as his personal bodyguard – and became a multimillionaire. Through the shock, excitement and horror we follow our laconic and entertaining escort as he retraces his wartime footsteps and revives memories of those savage yet sometimes strangely happy days in a memoir poignant with humour and pathos.

ABOUT THE AUTHOR

Alan Whicker's taut, forceful style gives a strong flavour of a forgotten world. After filming months of savagery and tragic loss amid heartbreaking displays of humanity and courage, he watched the total defeat of Hitler's 'invincible' Wehrmacht – then went to live in Venice in its first euphoric years of peace. As Churchill said of the broader Mediterranean canvas: few campaigns have had a finer culmination!

A year later, reluctantly leaving the Sea City for Austerity London, Whicker joined a Fleet Street news agency to travel the world as Foreign Correspondent. He returned to uniform as their War Correspondent in Korea. Later he moved across to television as one of the creators of the BBC's famous *Tonight* programme, in 1957. After ten years he left to join ITV's new Yorkshire Television, write four books and shoot some 300 *Whicker's Worlds* for both channels. Mentioned in Despatches for his war service, he has during a long career won most of television's notable awards and in 2005 was made a CBE.

WHAT THE REVIEWERS THOUGHT

'*Whicker's War* is simply brilliant . . . The iconic and utterly charming Alan Whicker recalls his own World War II experiences.'

Daily Mail

'It almost doesn't seem like a book at all, for so familiar is the Whicker economy of language and word rhythms that it is impossible to look over the opening paragraphs without hearing the Whicker voice reading the words out loud inside your head.'

Daily Telegraph

'Now the laid-back Whicker has retraced every step of the dramatic and emotional journey that he endured in his youth with a poignant story . . . with a perspective only a man of his pedigree could give. My bookshelf would certainly be a lot poorer without this written record. Inspired . . . and inspiring.'

Manchester Evening News

'Whicker captures something of what, we may guess, is the nature of warfare. A memorable piece of work . . .'

Glasgow Herald

'Alan Whicker's suave style was forged in a harsh arena. A vivid warm-hearted record.'

Sunday Telegraph

'The book is classic Whicker – well crafted, light and lucid, and full of informative detail, humour and pathos. It also contains wartime pictures taken by him, uncredited until now.'

Soldier

'The poignant prose, together with the stunning footage, results in a remarkable read.'

'One of the greatest TV icons of all time. His book makes remarkable reading.'

'Whicker's insights and delivery were brilliant – a series that unlocked the planet.'

'One of the outstanding broadcasters of the age and a reporter with notable gifts. Surrounded by carnage, corpses and the memory of lost friends, his familiar voice was as lilting and playful as ever, but laced with elegy ... It was beautifully written and delivered with such assurance that even the pauses were eloquent.'

'There's not a sentence wasted. Every word is to the point, and propels the narrative forward. Even the arch silences are golden.'

'Riveting – a marathon television series, now a compulsive and fascinating book . . .'

'Crisply written – a terrific read.' – RICHARD MADELEY
'Even I enjoyed it, and I don't really go for wars, much.' – JUDY FINNIGAN

WHICKER'S WAR

ALAN WHICKER

HarperCollins*Publishers*

HarperCollins*Entertainment*
An Imprint of HarperCollins*Publishers*
77–85 Fulham Palace Road,
Hammersmith, London W6 8JB

www.harpercollins.co.uk

This paperback edition 2006
1

First published in Great Britain by
HarperCollins*Entertainment* 2005

ISBN-10   0-00-720508-2
ISBN-13   978-0-00-720508-0

Set in ITC New Baskerville by
Rowland Phototypesetting Ltd, Bury St Edmund, Suffolk

Printed and bound in Great Britain by
Clays Ltd, St Ives plc

Dedicated to the men of
the Army Film and Photo Unit
who marched with me through Italy . . .

Also by the same author:

Within Whicker's World
Whicker's New World
Whicker's World Down Under
Whicker's World – Take 2!

CONTENTS

THAT EARLY SUMMER DAWN IN SICILY...

One man's war . . . a return to the invasion beaches and battlefields of Italy. A sentimental pilgrimage, I suppose, to places where I expected to die. Also a salute to those I marched alongside 60 years ago while growing up watching the world explode before the viewfinders of Army Film Unit battle-cameramen. In two years of savage warfare they gave a lot; some of them, everything.

As a teenage subaltern I'd volunteered for a new role in a new Army, and found myself out of the infantry but *in* to far more assault landings and battles than I'd expected. My belief that war could be anything except boring went unchallenged because our cameramen closely followed the action, indeed sometimes led it – though *that* was usually just poor map-reading . . .

I was part of the first great seaborne invasion. The Eighth Army was learning how to do it – and so, unfortunately, were the Germans.

The Italian campaign – one of the most desperate and bloody of World War II – was 660 days of fear and exhilaration. Churchill called it the Third Front. Life was strangely intense and sharp-focussed, yet every dramatic experience vanished like an exploding shell as we moved cheerfully along the cutting edge of war towards the next violent day.

The defence of Italy cost the Axis 556,000 casualties. The Allies lost 312,000 killed and wounded – and remember, this was The Overshadowed War. After Rome the Second Front captured our headlines and at Westminster, Lady Astor won the Hollow Laugh Award by calling us 'the D-Day Dodgers'.

As in the Great War, we subalterns had short sharp life expectations. Like those 19-year-old Battle of Britain pilots we learned to cope with this dismal forecast by being flip and jokey, but alert. It seemed to work for me – though more than half our camera crews were killed or damaged in some way while earning their Medals and Mentions.

As part of a massive Allied war fleet we joined this first great invasion of 2,700 ships and landing craft and on July 10 '43 struggled ashore on to Pachino beach at the bottom right-hand corner of Mussolini's island, expecting the worst. Around me on that early summer dawn in Sicily, 80,000 Eighth Army troops were also landing, and looking for a fight.

Our cameramen embedded in frontline units faced bitter warfare that I suspect few of today's young soldiers – let alone young civilians – could envisage in their worst nightmares. Among the perils in our path lay Churchill's gamble that failed, doomed by uncertain planning and leadership: the Anzio Bridgehead, where we all ceased to be young, where 250,000 soldiers were locked into a series of battles unique in the history of World War II. There in a few weeks of savage siege warfare 43,000 of us would be blown into history: 7,000 dead, 36,000 wounded or missing-in-action – but as we fought through Sicily such horrors lay ahead, unsuspected.

I stayed with Montgomery's desert army as it crossed the Straits of Messina to attack the Italian mainland. Then after Salerno went with the British/US Fifth Army to land 80 miles behind German lines, at Anzio. Our orders were to outflank Monte Cassino, cut Kesselring's supply lines, destroy his Tenth and Four-teenth armies and liberate Rome. That's all – in the afternoon we'd go to the cinema . . .

Breaking out of the bridgehead after 18 desperate weeks, the Fifth Army finally liberated Rome, though our war was lengthened by almost a year and many lives lost by the vanity of one insubordinate Allied General.

The Eighth fought on through the Apennines and the Gothic Line before sweeping down into the Po Valley to reach the Alps – and victory. Italy's Dictator Benito Mussolini and his mis-tress Clara Petacci were then hunted down and killed by their communist countrymen.

Those who doubted the strategic significance of our role in tying down 25 German divisions in Italy for two years – and the 55 divisions deployed around the Mediterranean – would have been heartened by Adolf Hitler's reaction. As we invaded Sicily and so pinned down one-fifth of Germany's military strength, he was controlling his wars from the *Wolfschanze,* his headquarters in East Prussia. He told his Generals that *Citadel,* the planned offensive against the Russians at Kursk, would be called off im-mediately. Their troops would go instead to the Italian front. That decision certainly did not make *our* task any lighter, but helping the Red Army was in fact our first victory – before firing a shot.

When we waded ashore on Sicily there were 2½ German divi-sions in Italy. Next year, as the Second Front opened, there were 24 – with three more on the way. We had made a difference. Even I made a small difference to the German SS by capturing several hundred of them, plus their General; I was also given a hidden fortune of many millions in hard currency – and then went to live in Venice. As Churchill said of our broader Mediterranean canvas: there have been few campaigns with a finer culmination!

Sixty years later I returned to Pachino to watch the sun rise over beaches where I had waded ashore up to the waist in warm Mediterranean and taken my first soggy steps on the long slog towards the Alps. I was then approaching two years of the worst – and a few of the very best – experiences of my life, when just staying alive was a celebration.

BEING SHOT WAS FOR ANOTHER DAY. . .

This odyssey began before the war with a Certificate A from the Officers' Training Corps at Haberdashers' Aske's School, Hampstead where, alarmed by the growing shadow of Hitler, we played at soldiering one night a week, went to summer camps and struggled with our exasperating puttees.

Came the war and I enlisted and was brushed by glory and instant power when made a Local Acting Unpaid Lance Corporal. Sewing on the lone stripe was a significant moment, rather like the ecstatic sight of that first bicycle. (I can still see mine leaning against the garden fence, all chrome and gleam. Compared with such utter bliss the sight of my first Bentley was as of dust).

I joined-up at the vast Ordnance Depot of Chilwell, outside Nottingham, and was selected as possible infantry officer material, which was worrying enough. The war had not been going well for us, and a moment's reflection would have warned me that if I wanted a long and happy life, the infantry was not the way to go.

In pursuit of that hazardous promotion, I drove north with my friend Harry Hamilton. He had a Ford Anglia and a hoarded

petrol ration. Along almost deserted wartime roads we headed
for Carlisle Castle and a Border Regiment training course which
would find out whether we were the right kind of cannon fodder.
With a hundred potential officers we shivered through an icy
January in two vast Crimean barrack rooms, sleeping on iron
bedsteads and queuing to unfreeze a couple of taps. The wind
whistled against cracked windows in a scene Florence Nightingale could have drifted through, the Lady with the Lamp looking
concerned about her poor boys.

Ham struck a considerable blow for comfort and the conser-
vation of life by chatting-up to some effect a girl who owned a
downtown snack bar. There behind gloriously steamy windows
we repaired for warmth and consolation from Army life which
seemed exactly the way it was in those boys' adventure books:
cheerful, but horrible.

As we were shivering on parade one day the Sergeant's
arm came down between Ham and me – and his half of the
squad turned left and marched towards the Officer Cadet
Training Unit at Dunbar in Scotland. The rest of us turned
right and headed for 164 OCTU at Barmouth, North Wales.
We did not meet again until after the war, when he was married
('I thought I was going to be killed and I wanted someone to
be sorry') and I was godfather to his first son. From then on
our lives diverged even more as he kept marrying, and I kept
not.

In the months of tough training which followed, the natural
splendour of Merioneth never got through to me. A mountain
merely meant something to run up with full pack, or stumble
around cursing on a night exercise. A river was to wade through,
a sun-dappled rocky chasm a place to cross while balancing on

a rope, white with fear. It was not until I returned to Dolgellau and Cader Idris after the war that I realised I had lived, head down and fists clenched, amid scenic magnificence.

Among Army skills which remained with me for life ... was how to avoid riding a motorcycle. I tried to manoeuvre my powerful beast up a one-in-two cliff path outside Harlech while the instructor insisted I stall the monster at the steepest point and then restart without losing equilibrium. That heart-bursting morning on a Welsh hillside wrestling a ton of vicious machinery to the ground put me off motorbikes for life. I have never ridden again. This must have spared me countless broken collarbones and torn ligaments. No experience is all bad.

As officer cadets, we were lorded-over on parade by the regulation Coldstream Guards regimental sergeant major straight from Central Casting: an enormous, bristling ramrod with foghorn voice. On our esplanade parade ground he spread terror and doubled platoons smartly into the sea and out again, sodden. Every day I tried to convince myself that, beneath it all, he was a dear old thing who loved his mother – but it wasn't easy. He put me on several charges for being lazy, unsoldierly and dreaming on parade. All these heinous offences were justified, though none was pursued or I might have suffered the ultimate disgrace of being RTU'd (Returned to Unit – who said the BBC invented initials?)

I also relished one unexpected moment of glory which redirected and established my military future. I had foolishly allowed myself to be badgered into volunteering to represent my Company at boxing – a lunatic decision deeply regretted at leisure. On the night of the execution I climbed reluctantly into the floodlights of Barmouth's packed town hall and glumly noted in the opposite corner a glowering opponent the size of a gorilla. This was a *light*-heavyweight? Around the ring – a place of blood and tears – sat the massed ranks, and the Unit's excited ATS girls. They were probably knitting.

I considered how to avoid total disgrace before the brass watching from the surrounding darkness who could make or break my military career. I had to forget all that stylish and gentlemanly dancing around, the Queensberry finesse and keeping-your-guard-up I had been taught in the school gym, but to tear into him regardless and go down swinging. At least he would finish me off quickly – and I might even save disgrace by getting a crafty one in, on the way down.

So at the bell I leapt from my corner and hurled myself desperately at the gorilla in a frenzy of hopeless determination, arms going like a windmill. It was the least scientific approach in boxing history. Within ten seconds of our violent clash in the centre of that brilliant ring, my enormous opponent was lying unconscious at my feet. Never again in an uninspired sporting career was I to feel such surprise, or receive such applause.

When I recovered from my amazement I was suitably modest – as though that sort of thing happened all the time. The gorilla was brought round with difficulty and carried away through the ropes with impatient disdain, towards some tumbril. The ATS didn't even bother to look up.

You can achieve quite a lot in ten seconds, and my reputation as a quiet killer with fists of iron spread through the unit. The Commanding Officer called me in to take a thoughtful look at this unexpected whirlwind in his midst. The girls in the Mess hall giggled at their mean street fighter and gave me larger portions, for Barmouth was a tiny coastal town miles from any excitement. Even the drill sergeants spoke to me approvingly – and that's unnatural. The RSM shouted no deafening threats for several days, and the rest of the Company 'D' backed away politely when I approached the tea urn.

However, retribution was not to be avoided: the Finals were already being advertised. Next Saturday night my aggressive bluff would be called. I was about to blow my reputation on the biggest night of the sporting season before Judges measuring me as possible Officer material. I briefly considered desertion, but finally and with growing concern went reluctantly back to the town hall wondering which ferocious man-mountain would emerge to wreak terrible revenge upon an upstart pretending to be a boxer.

My seconds bravely urged their champion to Go In and Kill Him, whoever he was. They only had me to lose, and there were plenty more where I came from. Once again I climbed glumly through the ropes and towards the scaffold, into a brilliance where no secrets could be hidden. I knew that this time my tactics would be no surprise. I should have to dance-around like a pro, and *box*. There was a price to pay for all that limelight. I resolved to sell my life as dearly and quickly as possible, and then step back into the shadows again. Barmouth had an efficient little hospital.

I looked around anxiously for my nemesis. The stool opposite was empty – a stage-managed delay, no doubt, to increase the suspense. We waited. It stayed empty. The pitiless ATS, hungry for more blood, were getting restless.

It slowly dawned upon me that I had underestimated my own publicity. My opponent, evidently a man who believed what he heard, had Gone Sick. His strategic withdrawal on medical grounds gave me a walkover. I received another ovation even more undeserved than the first and instantly retired from boxing forever, undefeated. Quit fast, is my theory, while you're ahead and uninjured.

I remain convinced the reason I walked through OCTU with high marks and emerged as a teenage officer was due, not to conscientious study or aptitude, not to all that square-bashing, sweat and effort – but to one lucky Saturday night punch that connected.

Since my Father's family came from Devon I was commissioned into 'The Bloody Eleventh' of the Line, the Devonshire Regiment. Feeling chipper and dashing in my service dress and gleaming Sam Browne, with that hard-won Pip on my shoulder, I'd stride through Mayfair, acknowledge a few salutes and be perfectly happy with my lot. Being shot was for another day.

Uplifted, I left my first-class Great Western carriage and reported for duty to the regimental Adjutant at Plymouth's Crownhill Barracks. To my disappointment he was not a fearsome Regular polo player with rows of brave ribbons, but a burbling beery ex-Territorial from Fleet Street, of all places. I felt he was the wrong sort of High Priest, playing in the wrong game. There may be nothing lower than a Second Lieutenant, but every volunteer needs a dashing role model.

However when I returned to my quarters, a batman had unpacked my kit, laid out the service dress, repolished buttons and Sam Browne, and run my bath. I had recently been living the roles of bored Lance Corporal, then weary Cadet. Now I had become overnight an Officer and a Gentleman. A little glory, with no visible risk. The war was never as good as that again, *ever.*

I savoured the moment. It seemed that running up all those mountains had been time well spent – despite the current prospect, as an infantry platoon commander, of the Army's shortest lifespan. I went for a snifter with the other chaps in the Mess, as we always say.

Soon after those triumphant moments in Plymouth, I prepared to pay the piper: Movement orders came through and I was suddenly a reinforcement, reporting to an unknown regiment in training at a remote place called Alloa. This had an undulating hula-hula lilt about it, like a magical posting to some romantic Polynesian isle. Could Whicker's Luck be holding?

No, it could not. Alloa turned out to be, not an exotic South Seas greeting but a grey and mournful Scottish industrial town in Clackmannanshire. The Battalion of East Surreys billeted in its sad empty houses was route-marched through the rain around Stirling. The Mess was a damp pub, the senior officers Regular wafflers, the NCOs morose, the men despairing. As one of the newer Crusaders, I found the atmosphere unjolly.

Depression grew. The solitary bright spot was my mandatory embarkation leave, after which our troopship would sail out across the Irish Sea to face the mines and submarines that were decimating Britain's remaining fleets and then, if we survived, the German army. We would be last seen steaming, it was believed, to Africa.

Before leaving Home and Mother for ever I was anxious to get a little mileage on the social scene out of my brand new service dress and lone pip. The journey back to London in a dark freezing wartime train offered standard depression, but next day came a welcome invitation to a farewell lunch at 67 Lombard Street given for me by an uncle, a City banker with Glyn Mills, to celebrate my elevation to elegant cannon-fodder. It was a pleasant meal. It also probably saved my life.

The other guest happened to be a Whitehall Warrior, a daunting blaze of red tabs and crowns and ribbons from the War Office who, over the port and Stilton, mentioned that one of his brand new units was looking for a young officer with news sense to join the Army's first properly-organized combat Film Unit which was about to leave for some hazardous secret landing in enemy territory. Could I, he wondered, could I direct sergeant-cameramen in battle? There would be a lot of action.

It took me a nanosecond to volunteer for this unknown

experience, anywhere at any time. It sounded like adventurous suicide – but it *was* stylish.

I returned to poor grey Alloa and its sullen soldiers, clutching a glimmer of hope amid their mass dejection. Next day the War Office offered me the posting. It was a decisive redirection, and an escape. I would be going into action before the East Surreys, but not *with* them. If I had to go and fight an enemy, I did at least want to get along with my own side.

A LONG LIFE WAS NOT IN THE SCRIPT . . .

So Whicker's War started prosaically in a black cab driving through empty streets towards the Hotel Great Central at Marylebone Station, then the London District Transit Camp. It was the first of many millions of travel miles around Whicker's World, though this time I was heading hopefully into the unknown and wondering what the hell was about to hit me.

At the reception desk I asked for AFPU. The corporal clerk checked his long list. 'Army Field Punishment Unit, Sir?'

'No,' I said, doubtfully. Surely the General had not tricked me? 'At least – I hope not.'

All was well. AFPU was assembling and preparing for embarkation. As far as I was concerned, there was no hurry – the West End would do fine for a few weeks, or more. Then we'd see about Africa or wherever.

One of my first Army Film and Photo Unit duties seemed close enough to Field Punishment. As the newest, youngest and greenest officer, I was instructed to give the whole unit an illustrated lecture on venereal disease and the dangers of illicit sex in foreign climes, a subject on which I was not then fully informed. The order that someone had to lay an Awful Warning on the Unit before it went to war had come amid masses of bumf from Headquarters and been passed down the line to be side-stepped with a hearty laugh by every available officer ... before stopping at the least significant.

A callow youth, but aging fast, I faced that parade of world-weary 35-year-old family men who seemed like knowing and experienced uncles. There were a few grizzled Regulars who at various postings around the world had obviously looked into the whole subject quite closely. It was not an easy moment. However, I gave them the benefit of my inexperience and they were most tolerant, listening as though I was telling them something new. Well, it was new to me.

The Great Central was plush and comfortable, after field kitchens and empty billets in Cumbria. I passed some mornings drilling our assorted band of cameramen in Dorset Square, NW1. Fresh from the ministrations and ferocity of a Guards RSM at OCTU, I was quite shocked by their casual and unmilitary bearing – and they didn't much care for mine, either. However I shouted a lot, and they fell into some sort of shape.

I was told to take them on a route march. I always found this a boring and pointless exercise so led them, not round and round Regents Park, but through such wartime bright lights as remained in the West End. Down Edgware Road to Marble Arch, where traffic waited while we crossed haughtily into Park Lane, then left for Piccadilly, up the hill, past the Ritz and left again into Bond Street. Such a route brightened the tedium of the march for us all; at least we could look into the shop windows as we strode past.

It would have been ideal for Christmas shopping, had the shops anything to sell and my Army pay been better than a few shillings a week. We were doubtless contravening a stack of regulations but even wartime Oxford Street was more visually entertaining than the country lanes around Dolgellau.

We were commanded by Major Hugh St Clair Stewart, a large gawky and humorous man who after the war, returned, quite suitably, to Pinewood to direct Morecambe and Wise and Norman Wisdom film comedies. Some of our sergeants were professional cameramen, others bus drivers and insurance clerks, salesmen and theatrical agents. All had been through Army basic training. 'I'd rather have soldiers being cameramen,' said Major Stewart, 'than cameramen trying to be soldiers, because one day they may have to put down their cameras and pick up rifles.' So they did.

At the start of World War II in the autumn of 1939, the War Office had sent one solitary accredited cameraman to cover the activities of the British Expeditionary Force in France. The powerful propaganda lessons of Dr Goebbels and Leni Riefenstahl had not been learned, so few pictures and no films emerged from that first unhappy battlefront. Neither the Guards' stand at Calais nor the desperate rescue from Dunkirk was covered pictorially – just a few haphazard shots, to be shown again and again. The Government had not awoken to the power of a picture to tell a truth or disguise a defeat, and the Treasury refused to find money to equip a film unit. Public relations still meant bald communiqués handed down from HQ, and parades when inspecting Royalty asked something unintelligible.

Two years later the power of Nazi propaganda upon morale at home and among neutral nations had begun to permeate Whitehall. After questions in Parliament, the War Office was finally permitted to provide some pictorial coverage for newspapers and newsreels and, equally important, for the Imperial War Museum and History. This belated reply to the Nazis' triumphant publicity was a grudging concession: the formation of a small active and responsible film unit. Its budget did not run to colour film which the Americans used, of course. Ours was to be a black-and-white war.

The Treasury also refused to pay for recording equipment, so we shall never hear the true sound of Montgomery leading the Eighth Army into battle, nor the fearful might of Anzio Annie, nor Churchill addressing the victorious First Army at Carthage.

The original Army Film Unit, 146 strong, had been sent to Cairo to cover the Middle East – then regarded as extending from Malta to Persia. It had 60 cameramen, half always to be on duty in the Western Desert. Their pictures of the Eighth Army in action began to filter home. They remain classic, as does their first feature film for the cinema, *Desert Victory*, edited at Pinewood from their collected footage. Churchill was proud to present a copy to President Roosevelt. Later there was *Tunisian Victory*. In this respect at least, the Treasury was edging slowly and reluctantly into the 20th century and becoming aware of the power of propaganda to influence the thoughts, decisions and spirit of nations.

War, we now know, is the most difficult event in the world to photograph – even with today's brilliant technology and miniaturisation. Audiences have grown accustomed to John Mills ice cold in Alex and John Wayne capturing a plaster Guadalcanal in close up and artificial sweat while smoke bursts go off over his shoulder and are dubbed afterwards in death-defying stereo. Just watch Tom Hanks storming Normandy. Terrifying. So viewers are not impressed by a tank in middle distance and a couple of soldiers hugging the dirt in foreground – even though at that moment real men may be shedding real blood.

Reality can be dull, unreality cannot afford to be; yet should a cameraman get close enough to war to make his pictures look real he is soon, more often than not, a dead cameraman.

The second film unit, which I was joining, was formed to cover the new southern warfront in North Africa and the threatened battlefields of Europe. To provide Britain and the world with an idea of the life and death of our armies at war, the No 2 Army Film and Photo Unit eventually took 200,000 black-and-white stills and shot well over half-a-million feet of film. We were busy enough.

To get those pictures, eight of the little band of 40 officers and sergeant-cameramen were killed and 13 badly wounded. They earned two Military Crosses, an MBE, three Military Medals, 11 Mentions in Despatches – and, eventually, a CBE. Today, any picture you see of the Eighth, Fifth or First Armies in action was certainly taken by these men.

The sergeant-cameramen worked under a Director – a Captain or Lieutenant – and travelled the war zones in pairs, with jeep and driver. Their cine footage and still pictures were collected as shot and returned to base for development, and transmission back to London. By today's standards their equipment was pathetic – any weekend enthusiast would be scornful. Each stills photographer was issued with a Super Ikonta – a Zeiss Ikon with 2.8 lens, yellow filter and lens hood. Each cine man covering for newsreels, films and television-to-be had an American De Vry camera in its box – a sort of king-size sardine tin – with 35mm, 2″ and 6″ lens. No zoom, no powerful telephoto lens, no sound equipment; effects would be dubbed in afterwards – usually to stirring or irritating music, with commentary written in London.

To get a picture of a shell exploding the cameraman needed to will one to land nearby as he waited, Ikonta cocked. If it had not been fatally close, he would shoot when smoke and dust allowed, otherwise the explosion which could have killed him would be invisible on film. A German tank had to be close and centre-frame before he could take a reasonable shot – by which time the tank might well take one too, more forcibly. A long life was not in the script. So, ill-equipped but confident, we went to war.

HIS MAJESTY GOT A WRONG NUMBER . . .

It certainly began badly for Britain. In 1940 France surrendered and we were driven out of Europe. Hitler ruled the Continent, Italy and Japan declared war upon us. Only in Africa did we eventually taste victory, at El Alamein and Tunis. But now in '43 we were starting our return journey to Europe in gathering strength alongside our new American ally.

The Army Film Unit approached the recapture of Europe by a rather circuitous route, it seemed. Small enough to start with, it had been split into even tinier segments as we went to war alone, or in pairs, and approached Hitler's European fortress surreptitiously. We knew that convoy sailings were top secret, and at our Marylebone hotel faces now familiar would suddenly disappear without a word. There were no Going-Away parties.

When it came to my turn, I sailed from the Clyde one bleak January night in the 10,000-ton *Chattanooga City*, with a shipful of strangers. We still did not know where we were going, but it had to be towards warmer waters to the south. Our convoy formed up and we joined a mass of other merchantmen and a few escorting frigates and destroyers, heading out towards the

Atlantic and the threatening Bay of Biscay at the sedate pace of the slowest ship.

This did not seem reassuring, since the U-boats were still winning the Battle of the Atlantic. We had a lot of safety drills, though felt rather fatalistic about them. Convoys would never stop to pick up survivors after a ship had been torpedoed. The escorts would not even slow down – so why bother with life jackets? The outlook was grey, all round.

There must have been 30 ships in our convoy, but only a couple were torpedoed during the voyage. Both were outsiders, steaming at the end of their line – so seemingly easier targets, less well-protected. The U-boats attacked at night – the most alarming time – yet the convoy sailed on at the same slow steady speed as though nothing had happened. Our escorts were frantic – and the sea shuddered with depth charges as we sailed serenely into the night. Two shiploads of men had been left to their wretched fate in the darkness.

Our ship was basic transport, with temporary troop-carrying accommodation built within its decks. The Officers' Mess – one long table – was surrounded by bunks in cubicles. Meals, though not very good, were at least different, and plentiful. Most of the officers were American, so we passed much of the following days and nights playing poker. This was a useful education.

When we reached the Bay it was relatively peaceful, though with a heavy swell. On the blacked-out deck I clung-on and watched the moonlit horizon descend from the sky and disappear below the deck. After a pause it reappeared and climbed towards the sky again. I was stationary, but the horizon was performing very strangely.

We passed our first landfall at night – the breathtaking hulk of Gibraltar – without really believing we could fool the Axis telescopes spying from the Spanish coast and taking down our details. By now we knew we were heading for the exotic destination of Algiers. Its agreeable odour of herbs, spices and warm Casbah wafted out to sea to greet us.

In Algiers I rounded up our drivers and we collected the Unit's transport: Austin PUs – more than 20 of them. These 'personal utilities' were like small underpowered delivery vans, but comfortable enough for two. They saw us through the war until America's more warlike jeeps drove to the rescue. I had been told to deliver this motorcade to AFPU in a small town in the next country: Beja, in Tunisia, where we were becoming a Unit again.

I thought that having come all this way I ought to take a look at Sidi-Bel-Abbès to check-out the HQ of the Foreign Legion, but it was on the Moroccan side of Algeria, and the Legionnaires still uncertain whether they were fighting for us or against us. In Algiers I consoled myself in the cavernous Aletti bar with other officers heading for the war. Then we set off for Stif and Constantine. It was a lovely mountain drive on good roads in cool sunshine, with the enemy miles away.

The journey to recapture Europe was taking the new First Army longer than expected. Our push towards the Mediterranean ports of Tunisia, from where we planned to attack Europe, had been halted. Hitler was supporting the fading Afrika Korps to keep us away from his new frontiers. The enemy was now being reinforced every day by 1,000 fresh German troops from Italy. They flew in to El Aouina Airport at Tunis and joined the tired remainder of the Afrika Korps arriving across the Libyan Desert, just ahead of the Eighth Army.

At Beja we unloaded the supplies we had been carrying in our PUs and joined the rest of the Unit awaiting us in a small decrepit hotel. I had been carrying one particularly valued memento of peaceful days. It says something for the progress of technology when I reveal that this was a small portable handwound gramophone with a horn, as in His Master's Voice. It now seems laughably Twenties and charleston, but in those days there were no such things as miniature radios, of course, and great chunky wireless sets required heavy accumulators.

Unfortunately, the accompanying gramophone records I brought had not coped with the stressful voyage. The solitary survivor was good old Fats Waller singing *My Very Good Friend the Milkman.* On the flip side: *Your Feets Too Big.* We played this treasure endlessly, then passed him on to the Sergeants' Mess for the few cameramen still not placed with Army units. When they could stand him no longer he was joyfully received by the drivers. Fortunately Fats Waller's voice was not so delicate or finely-tuned an instrument that it lost much quality from constant repetition. I always hoped that one day I would be able to tell him how much one recording did for the morale of a small unit stranded amid the sand and scrub of North Africa.

The First Army had earlier been expected to occupy Tunis and Bizerte without difficulty, but instead lost Longstop Hill and was almost pushed back from Medjez-el-Bab. A major attack was planned to make good that defeat and capture the remaining enemy forces in North Africa. Leading the thrust for Tunis would be two armoured divisions. I went to join a photogenic squadron of Churchill tanks, awaiting action.

The Churchill was our first serious tank, developed before the war. It weighed 39 tons and with a 350hp engine could reach 15mph, on a good day. It originally had a two-pounder gun, which must have seemed like a peashooter poking out of all that steel. Then in '42 its manufacturer Vauxhall Motors installed a six-pounder. In '73 this was replaced by a 75mm, making it at last a serious contender – though the German Tiger we were yet to meet weighed 57 tons and had an 88mm. Throughout the entire war German armour was always just ahead of us. We never met on equal terms. However, we had heard how Montgomery had run the Panzers out of Libya, so were optimistic about our chances before Tunis.

For my cine-cameraman partner I asked Sergeant Radford to join me. Back in our old Marylebone days Radford had been the main protester against marching and drilling with the rest of the Unit in Dorset Square. He always seemed a bit of a barrack-room lawyer, so I thought I should carry the load rather than push him into partnership with some less stroppy sergeant. With a precise, fastidious and pedantic manner – before the war I believe he had been in Insurance – Radford was a great dotter of i's and crosser of t's, but I suspected where it mattered he was a good man. In fact on the battlefront and away from Dorset Square we soon came to terms. He was a splendid and enthusiastic cameraman, and would go after his pictures like a terrier.

On our first battle outside Tunis, some Churchills suffered the mechanical problems they inherited from the original 100 Churchills remaining in the Army after Dunkirk, and broke down. The day did not go well.

You don't remember events too clearly, after a battle. It's all too fast and fierce and frightening – but I do recall seeing Radford going forward clinging on to the back of a tank, as though riding a stallion into the fray.

Being on the outside looking in, is never a wise position in war. Nevertheless after a busy day on Tunisian hillsides, we both found ourselves on the lower slopes of Longstop Hill when the final attack was called off. I was mightily relieved to see him again, exhausted but in good shape.

Next day the Commanding Officer drew me aside. He was a

smiling Quorn countryman who would have been happier riding to hounds. Our enthusiasm, he said, had been 'a good show'. That was a relief, since I gathered we had been seen as a bit long-haired and effete. At least the Regiment's worst suspicions had not been confirmed ... To be complimented by a CO of such style and panache was accolade enough; then he added that when life calmed down he was going to put us both in for gongs. That seemed a satisfactory way for a Film Unit to start its war and a reminder that we were not there to take pictures of parades.

When the battle for Tunis resumed next dawn German gunners concentrated upon our lead tank. The CO was the first man to be killed.

The elusive quality of battlefield behaviour is well-known: bravery unnoticed, medals unawarded ... because no one was there to see. Yet Radford's behaviour in the face of the enemy had been seen by a senior officer who, when we had asked permission to join his tanks, thought we might be a nuisance. At least on our first day in battle we had not let down that most gallant gentleman.

Yet in truth, we were not in the hero business. Our CO regularly reminded us that no ephemeral picture was worth a death or an injury. This did not stop the braver cameramen risking their lives. (The General who led the British forces in a later war in the Gulf, Sir Peter de la Billiere, has reminded us, 'The word "hero" has become devalued. Nowadays it's applied to footballers and film stars, which does a disservice to people who have risked their lives for others.')

So we covered the slow advance through Tunisia. It was our first experience of fighting alongside the Americans. Totally unblooded, they were quite unequal even to General Rommel's beaten army at Kairouan and the Kasserine Pass, suffering 6,000 battle casualties and a demoralizing major defeat in their first engagement of the war. The Germans were amazed at the quantity and quality of the US equipment they captured intact.

In April '43, after observing the battle for Tunisia, the Allied Commander, General Sir Harold Alexander, found the US troops 'soft, green and quite untrained'. He reported to the Chief of the Imperial General Staff, General Sir Alan Brooke: 'There are millions of them elsewhere who must be living in a fool's paradise. If this handful of divisions here are their best, the value of the rest may be imagined.'

Anglo-American relations became even more strained following a brusque signal from the Allied Tactical Air Commander, Air Vice Marshal Sir Arthur Coningham, to Lieutenant General George S. Patton Jr, concerning close air support. It told the pugnacious American that his II Corps was not battle-worthy. That did it.

The Allied Air Commander-in-Chief Sir Arthur Tedder averted a major crisis by sending Coningham to apologize personally to Patton, however accurate his assessment. I have never been able to discover details of that interesting meeting. At AFHQ the incident was seen as so serious that the Allied Commander-in-Chief General Eisenhower prepared to resign.

Relations could only get better, as indicated by the later effective emergence of the explosive Patton, pearl-handled revolvers, polished helmet and all – hence 'Gorgeous George'. This aggressive cavalryman became the Allies' most effective commander of armoured formations.

After their victory at Kairouan the German advance threatened

AFPU's new billet at Sedjenane. This was in the local brothel – by then out of action. Its only remaining attraction was a fine double bed, and when our cameramen joined the US Army in their tactical withdrawal they were anxious to retain this new-found luxury with its comforting peacetime aura. Unfortunately AFPU's available transport by then was one motorcycle.

The local Arab population was impressed, and a solemn procession carried the bed along the only street to a safer billet – which next day was destroyed by an enemy shell. This however was a hardy bed which had obviously seen a lot of action; it survived and was moved yet again into the safest place around: a deep mine.

When the German advance continued the bed had to be sacrificed as a spoil of war. Later Sedjenane was recaptured – and there stood the long-suffering AFPU double bed, none the worse for recent German occupation apart from a slight green mould. Yet somehow its erotic appeal had diminished . . .

Tunis was the first major city to be liberated by the Allies during the war, the first streets full of deliriously happy people when men proffered hoarded champagne and pretty girls their all – a scene to be repeated many times in the freed cities of Europe. The crowd around us in the Avenue Jules Ferry was so jammed and ecstatic we could not move. I was standing on the bonnet of my car filming laughing faces and toasting 'Vive la France' when I saw Sidney Bernstein, even then a cinema mogul. He had arrived from the Ministry of Information bringing *In Which We Serve* and other gallant war films to show the liberated people, and now faced a different sort of film fan: 'How do I get the French out of my car?' he grumbled.

One of my cameramen apologised in his dope sheet for the

quality of his pictures: 'I have been kissed so many times by both women and *men* that it really is difficult to concentrate . . .' War can be hell.

On May 12, '43, the enemy armies in Africa capitulated; 250,415 Germans and Italians laid down their arms at Cap Bon. General von Arnim surrendered to a Lieutenant Colonel of the Gurkhas, explaining that his officers were 'most anxious' to surrender only to the British. We took pictures of thousands of Afrika Korpsmen driving themselves happily into captivity past one of their oompah-pah brass bands playing 'Roll out the barrel' inside a crowded prison cage.

For a Victory celebration at a time when the British Army was noticeably short of victories, Prime Minister Churchill flew into El Aouina airport outside Tunis and drove straight to the first Roman amphitheatre at Carthage to congratulate his First Army, then preparing for its next target – presumably Italy.

To cover this historic celebration we posted photographers all over the amphitheatre. Captain Harry Rignold, our most experienced cameraman, was up on the top tier with our lone Newman Sinclair camera and the unit's pride: a 17-inch telephoto lens. We also needed close-up stills of Churchill, so I was sitting on the large rocks right in front of the stage – in the orchestra stalls – feeling rather exposed before that military mass. Indeed the task proved more difficult than expected.

In the brilliant African sun Churchill climbed on stage and with hands dug into pockets in his best bulldog style, faced 3,000 of his troops. Next to him stood the Foreign Secretary Anthony Eden and the ultimate red-tabs: General Sir Alan Brooke, CIGS, with the victorious First Army Commander, Lieutenant General Kenneth Anderson. Their only prop was a small wooden table covered by a Union Jack. It was not Riefenstahl's stage-managed Nuremberg and would win no awards, but it was at least naturally splendid.

The troops roared their welcome. Churchill seemed surprised and delighted at a reception made even more dramatic by perfect Roman acoustics. 'Get a picture of that,' he said, spotting me in the stalls busily focusing on him. He waved towards the amphitheatre behind me. 'Don't take me – take *that.*'

I wanted to explain that several of our cameramen were at that moment filming the cheering mass as he stood at its heart, that he was the star and a picture of a lot of soldiers without him was not new or significant . . . when once more that famous voice ordered, 'Get a picture of that.' He was clearly not used to saying things twice – certainly not to young lieutenants. For a moment I wavered. General Anderson, breathing heavily, took a step forward and my court martial flashed before me. 'Take a picture of *that!*' he snapped.

I took a picture of that.

I had to wait until Churchill was well into his panegyric before I could turn and sneak my shot of him amidst his victorious army. Afterwards he walked out to his car, took off his pith helmet and waved it from the top of his stick, gave the V sign and drove away with his Generals. *That* bit of our war had been won.

There was a brief pause while the armies digested their victory and prepared for the next invasion, and at the beginning of May '43 our life became almost social. It was spring and, what's more, we were still alive. We requisitioned a villa at Sidi Bou Saïd, near Carthage. It overlooked the Bay of Tunis and had indoor sanitation, to which we had grown unaccustomed.

My Austin utility was still bent from the weight of jubilant Tunisiennes, so to support our celebrations I had liberated a splendid German staff car, an Opel Kapitan in Wehrmacht camouflage. We were not supposed to use unauthorised transport, so along the German bonnet we craftily painted some imaginary but official-looking numbers – my home telephone number, if you must know.

The start of it all . . . Directing our first picture sequence in the murky back streets of wartime Holborn, before we sailed for the Mediterranean. This assignment from Pinewood Studios was to film church bells ringing a Victory peal. They were a couple of years early – but it worked out all right in the end . . .

Above: Ready to go!
Identity Card picture.

Top right and above: Invading Italy!

Above: We are shepherded onto the landing beaches by the Royal Navy.

Below: The Landing Ship Tank was the star of every invasion beach around the world . . .

Above: War! What approaching death must look like to an unlucky soldier: the final German shell explodes . . .

Below: Infantrymen clear a village, covered by a Bren gunner and a couple of riflemen.

Above: The Royal Artillery's 155mm gun goes into action.

Above: Throughout the length of Italy German engineers delayed our advance by blowing every bridge in our path.

Right: The Royal Engineers' first solution sometimes looked slightly insecure . . .

Left: Briefing AFPU cameramen on how we'll cover the next battle. The regulation De Vry cine-camera, next to water bottle.

Above inset: Sergeant Radford had been filming a Regiment of Churchill tanks in action. His film stock is replenished . . .

Above: . . . and the footage he has shot is taken by dispatch rider back to the Developing Section at base.

Right: We were issued with Super Ikontas, inadequate cameras without telephoto lenses.

Left: Celebrating our Sicilian victory at Casa Cuseni in Taormina, while awaiting the invasion of Italy. We even had time to perfect the Unit's 'Silly Walks' – some 30 years before Monty Python.

Below: I can't remember the reason for this outburst of warrior's relaxation. (It was in the morning, so demon vino was no excuse). Excessive exuberance, perhaps.

Above: The Mess dining room, 60 years ago. Today, unchanged, even the pictures are the same . . .

Left: . . . as is the terrace. In those days . . .

Below: . . . and now.

I thought we had got away with it until my contraband car was admired at embarrassing length – by King George VI. As I stood to attention before His Majesty, it seemed cruel that the only finger of suspicion should be Regal.

The King had just arrived in Tunis at the start of his Mediterranean tour with Sir James Grigg and Sir Archibald Sinclair. In the welcoming cortège at the airport he spotted my unusual Afrika Korps convertible and pointed it out to General Alexander: 'That's a fine car,' said His Majesty. 'Very fine.' The General, compact and elegant, studied it for what seemed a long time. Following his eyeline, all I could see was my phone number growing larger under Royal inspection.

'Yes Sir,' he said, finally. 'A German staff car captured near here by this young officer, I should imagine.' He gave me a thoughtful look – then they all drove away in a flurry of flags and celebration. I took the phoney car in the opposite direction, quite fast.

It transported me in comfort for some happy weeks until, parked one afternoon outside the office of the *Eighth Army News* in Tunis it was stolen by – I discovered years later – a brother officer from the Royal Engineers. Stealing captured transport from your own side has to be a war crime.

The King sailed to Malta in the cruiser *Aurora*, and we scrambled to reach Tripoli by road in time to cover his reception there. The Libyan capital was a cheerless contrast to exuberant Tunis, where they loved us. Streets had to be cleared of sullen Tripolitanians who evidently much preferred Italian occupation. I waited for the arrival ceremony in an open-air café and for the first time heard the wartime anthem 'Lili Marlene', played for British officers by a bad-tempered band. It felt strange to be unwelcome – after all, we *were* liberators.

The immaculate King was greeted by General Montgomery,

who as usual dressed down for the occasion: smart casual – shirt, slacks, black Tank Corps beret, long horsehair flywhisk.

Filming with us was our new commanding officer, Major Geoffrey Keating, who became a close friend until his death in 1981. Keating had cut a brave figure in the desert; his photographs and those of his cameramen first made the unusual and unknown Montgomery a national hero. In truth, with high-pitched voice and uneasy birdlike delivery, he was a man with little charm or charisma. He seemed unable to relate to his troops, though on occasion he would try – proffering packets of cigarettes abruptly from his open Humber. However, he *was* a winner – and because of AFPU was the only publicly recognisable face in the whole Eighth Army.

Montgomery would never start a battle he was not sure of winning, so his men – who had suffered more than their ration of losing Generals – followed him cheerfully. His main military principle was that Army commanders should plan battles – not staff officers and *certainly* not politicians. Unsurprisingly he was not too popular with his Commander, Winston Churchill, who since Gallipoli and South Africa had longed to control troops in action.

On top of all his achievements, Churchill had a lifetime yearning to become a warrior-hero. He did not hide this improbable dream. An early biographer wrote, 'He sees himself moving through the smoke of battle, triumphant, terrible, his brow clothed with thunder, his Legions looking to him for victory – and not looking in vain. He thinks of Napoleon; he thinks of his great ancestor the Duke of Marlborough . . .'

After the Gallipoli disaster in the Great War he did achieve a few months of frontline battle as a Lieutenant Colonel commanding a Rifle battalion in France. Ever afterwards he looked for another commanding role on some dramatic battlefront. At last Anzio emerged – the assault landing no one wanted. We who went there soon understood *why*.

Keating had flown to London with his victorious General and returned with the news that, as expected, we were about to assault Italy. The Eighth Army, the US Seventh Army and the 1st Canadian Corps would first attack Sicily, that hinge on the door to Europe, and then pursue the enemy north towards the Alps.

Invasion forces for Operation *Husky* were gathering at Mediterranean ports from Alexandria to Gibraltar, so I left hateful Tripoli with a convoy of new AFPU jeeps just off a ship from the States and headed flat-out across the desert back to Sousse, from where our invasion fleet would sail.

At the Libyan border we slipped off Mussolini's tarmac road on to the sandy track through Tunisia. This had been deliberately left in poor condition by the French to slow Mussolini's armoured columns – or that was their excuse. Through Medenine and the Mareth Line the hot desert which had so recently been a desperate battlefield and seen the last hurrah of the Afrika Korps now stood quiet and empty. It was dotted with the hulks of tanks and armoured cars, and the occasional rough wooden cross: a few sad square feet of Britain or America, Italy or Germany.

Sousse was bustling as XIII Corps got ready to fight again. We placed cameramen with the battalions which were to lead the invasion. I was to land with the famous 51st Highland Division which had battled 2,000 miles across North Africa from El Alamein. The Scots are rather useful people to have on your side if you're expecting to get into a fight, and I was promised a noisy time.

Before the armada sailed I dashed back to Sidi Bou Saïd with secret film we had taken of the invasion preparations for dispatch to London. Coated with sand and exhausted, I arrived at our requisitioned hillside villa to find a scene of enviable tranquillity: on the elegant terrace overlooking the Bay, AFPU's new Adjutant was giving a dinner party.

At a long table under the trees sat John Gunther, the *Inside Europe* author then representing the *Blue* radio network of America, Ted Gilling of the *Exchange Telegraph* news agency who was later to become my first Fleet Street Editor, and other Correspondents. In the hush of the African dusk, the whole scene looked like Hollywood.

After a bath I joined them on the patio as the sun slipped behind the mountains, drinking the red wine of Carthage and listening to cicadas in the olive groves. In a day or two I was to land on a hostile shore, somewhere. Would life ever again be as tranquil and contented and *normal*? Would I be appreciating it – or Resting in Peace?

Watching the moon rise over a calm scene of good fellowship, it was hard not to be envious of this rear-echelon going about its duties far from any danger and without dread of what might happen in the coming assault landing. Dinner would be on the table tomorrow night as usual, and bed would be cool and inviting. I had chosen military excitement – but forgotten that in the Army the hurly-burly of battle always excluded comfort and well-ordered certainty. I took another glass or two of Tunisian red.

Back in Sousse next day, envy forgotten, I boarded my LST – the Landing Ship Tank. This was the first use of the British-designed American-built amphibious craft that was to be the star of every invasion across the world. A strange monster with huge jaws – a bow that opened wide and a tongue that came down slowly to make a drawbridge. Only 328 feet in length, powered by two great diesels, it could carry more than 2,000-tons of armour or supplies through rough seas and with shallow draught, ride right up a beach, vomit its load onto the shore, and go astern. Disembarking troops or armour was the most dangerous part of any landing, so was always fast. Sometimes, frantic.

Anchored side by side this great fleet of LSTs filled the harbour. Once aboard I wandered around sizing-up my fellow passengers. They were all a bit subdued, that evening. An assault landing against our toughest enemy was rather like awaiting your execution in the morning; there was not much spare time for trivial thoughts or chatter.

We were in the first wave, and the approaching experience would surely be overwhelming enough, even if we lived through it. During that soft African twilight there was little shared laughter.

THEY ASKED FOR IT — AND THEY WILL NOW GET IT . . .

The fleet sailed at dusk on July 9, '43, setting off in single file, then coming up into six lines. The senior officer on each ship paraded his troops and briefed them on the coming assault landing. We were to go in at Pachino, the fulcrum of the landing beaches at the bottom right-hand corner of Sicily.

Back in the wardroom our Brigadier briefed his officers. Then, traditionally, we took a few pink gins. The intention now was to knock Italy out of the war. We were off to kill a lot of people we did not know, and who we might not dislike if we *did* meet; and of course, we would try to stop them killing us. 'Could be a thoroughly sticky landing chaps,' he said, awkwardly.

I have often wondered whether scriptwriters and novelists imitate life, or do we just read the book, see the movie – and copy *them*, learning how we ought to react in dramatic and unusual situations? Noël Coward showed us, with *In Which We Serve;* no upper lip was ever stiffer. Ealing Studios followed. Even Hollywood, in a bizarre way, looked at *Gunga Din* and the *Bengal Lancers*. We all knew about *Action!* but in Sicily, in real life, no one was going to shout *Cut!*

The armada sailed on, blacked-out and silent but for the softly swishing sea. Then the desperate night upon which so much depended changed its mind and blew up a sudden Mediterranean storm so severe (we learned later) that it convinced the enemy we could not invade next morning – but which surprisingly I do not remember at all. When you are braced for battle it does wipe away lesser worries – like being seasick, or drowning.

The storm blew itself out as abruptly as it had arrived, and I went back on deck to find we were surrounded by other shadowy craft with new and strange silhouettes which had assembled during the night. Ships had been converging from most ports in the Mediterranean, from Oran to Alex, to carry this Allied army to the enemy coast.

In the moonlight I tried to sleep on unsympathetic steel, fully dressed and sweating, lifebelt handy. Then around 4am the troops came cursing and coughing up out of the fug below decks into the grey dawn, buckling equipment and queuing for the rum ration.

Some took a last baffled glance at an unexpected Army pamphlet just distributed: 'A Soldier's Guide to Sicily'. Hard to keep a straight face. It was full of useful hints, like the opening hours of cathedrals, how to introduce yourself, and why you should not invade on early-closing day. It could have been a cut-price package cruise of the Med if the food had been more generous and we had not been preparing to break into Hitler's fortress.

The Army Commander, General Montgomery, brought us back to reality. It is now easy to mock his resonant 'good-hunting!' calls to action, but they were penned more than sixty years ago, pre-television when reality had not begun to intrude upon Ealing Studios' rhetoric.

Montgomery told us: 'The Italian overseas Empire has been exterminated; we will now deal with the home country. The Eighth Army has been given the great honour of representing the British Empire in the Allied force which is now to carry out this task. Together we will set about the Italians in their own country in no uncertain way; they came into this war to suit themselves and they must now take the consequences; they asked for it, and they will now get it . . .'

He concluded: 'The eyes of our families and in fact of the whole Empire will be on us once the battle starts. We will see they get good news and plenty of it. Good luck and good hunting in the home country of Italy.'

Wandering around the decks, I saw no one showing anxiety, no animosity, no heroics. There was too much to think about. Fear is born and grows in comfort and security, which were not available at that moment in the Med. Or perhaps we were all acting?

Action! was at first light on July 10 '43 when British troops returned to Europe, wading ashore on to the sandy triangular rock that is Sicily. It was the first great invasion. *Cut!* came two years later, and was untidy.

The Eighth Army had 4½ divisions, the US Seventh Army 2½. Along the coast to our left the Americans and 1st Canadian Division were landing. The 231 Independent Brigade from Malta, the 50th and the 5th Divisions hit the beaches in an arc north towards Syracuse. Some 750 ships put 16,000 men ashore, followed by 600 tanks and 14,000 vehicles. We were covered, they assured us, by 4,000 aircraft. I saw very few – and most of those were Luftwaffe. I presumed, and hoped, that the RAF and the USAAF were busy attacking enemy installations and airfields elsewhere, to ease our way ashore.

While driving the enemy out of Africa the Eighth Army had

settled the conflict in Tunisia by capturing the last quarter-of-a-million men of the Afrika Korps. Many could have escaped to Sicily had Hitler not ordered another fight to the death. At the end most were sensible, and surrendered – including General von Arnim with his 5th Panzer Army.

The triumphant conclusion of the North African campaign left the Allies with powerful armies poised for their next great offensive. President Roosevelt, unhappy on the sidelines, was determined to get his troops into action *somewhere,* and Italy provided the best targets available while building-up forces and experience for the Second Front. Despite their African victory the Allies were not yet dominant nor confident enough to invade France – certainly not the Americans, with little or no battle experience.

So at Churchill's insistence we were to attack 'the soft underbelly of Fortress Europe'. That's what *he* called it. In the event, it was not as soft as advertised; indeed, it grew almost too hard to resist. After only just avoiding being pushed back into the sea a couple of times, we became resigned to Churchill's brave optimism.

The strategic intention was to knock Italy out of the war and to tie down the 25 German occupying divisions – 55 in the whole Mediterranean area – which could otherwise have changed the balance of power on Russian battlefields or turned the coming Second Front in Normandy into a catastrophe.

The Germans were now compelled to withdraw units from their armies around Europe to reinforce the Italian front: the Hermann Goering Division from France, the 20th Luftwaffe Field Division from Denmark, the 42nd Jäger and 162nd Turko-man Divisions from the Balkans, the 10th Luftwaffe Field Division from Belgium . . . were the first to leave their positions and head for Italy. By drawing some of the Wehrmacht's finest units into battle, we supported Germany's hard-pressed enemies everywhere.

Mussolini's Fascist regime had already been demoralised by the loss of its African empire and army, and if we could now drive Italy out of the war our frontier would be the Alps, and the Mediterranean route to the Middle and Far East secure. To defend Sicily with its 600 miles of coastline, the Italian General Alfredo Guzzoni had twelve divisions – ten Italian and only two German: 350,000 men, including 75,000 Germans. With Kesselring's instant reaction, by the end of August seven fully equipped German divisions were attacking us in Sicily.

To clear our sea route to this battlefield and obtain a useful airfield, the Allies had first attacked Pantelleria, a tiny volcanic island 60 miles south of Sicily. It surrendered without a shot being fired on June 11 after severe bombing, and was found to have a garrison of 11,000 troops – a ready-made prisoner-of-war camp and an indication that Mussolini's strategic planning could be haphazard. The only British casualty during this invasion was one soldier bitten by a mule.

Though the Allies dropped 6,570 tons of bombs on that Mediterranean rock the garrison suffered few casualties and only two of its 54 gun batteries were knocked out. Such pathetic results did not lead Allied High Command to question the efficacy of future saturation bombing.

Our landing in Sicily was also preceded by the first Allied airborne operation of any size. A parachute regiment of the 82nd Airborne Division and a British Glider Brigade were flown from Kairouan, Tunisia, in some 400 transport aircraft and 137 gliders. This daring night operation was the first ever attempted. It was not a success.

Poorly-trained pilots had to face dangerously high winds, so only twelve gliders landed near their objective, and 47 crashed into the sea; they had been cast off too early by their American towing aircraft. The fact that our aerial armada was fired-on by Allied naval vessels did not help. The 75 Dakotas also dropped the US paratroops far from their target of Gela, scattering them across Sicily.

The survivors of the Glider Force saved their part of the operation from complete disaster by causing some chaos among the defences around the Ponte Grande across the River Anapo. These elite troops removed all demolition charges from the bridge, enabling the 5th Division to drive straight across, head for Syracuse and occupy it that night with port installations little damaged.

So Sicily was a curtain-raiser for Europe's major airborne landing at Arnhem in September '44 – which was equally unwise and unsuccessful.

Otherwise the first great invasion was going well. Only four of our great fleet of some 3,000 ships in convoy had been torpedoed. Kesselring did not seem to have noticed our arrival. We learned later there was frenzy at the Field Marshal's HQ – but this did not show.

At Pachino our LST came to anchor offshore. A few enemy miss-and-run spotter aircraft roared over, too high for pictures. When it grew light we needed to get closer in, so with Sgt Radford, I thumbed a lift on a smaller Landing Craft Infantry. We slipped from that into the Med, struggling armpit-deep through the gentle breakers and holding our cameras high. The LCI Captain, a young Australian Lieutenant with whom during the tense dawn I had been considering life, the future and everything, this Ozzie very decently jumped into the sea and waded behind me, holding my back-pack full of unexposed film up out of the Med.

On the continent of Europe I took my first sodden steps on the long march towards the Alps. So far, so surprisingly good.

At that stage of the war nobody knew much about assault landings, about storming ashore and facing mines on the beaches and machine guns in pillboxes backed by mortars and artillery and bombers. Despite hesitant or invisible opposition, there was a new naked sensation. Standing tense on that soft warm beach and gazing around I was ready to burrow into the sand for protection. I felt exposed and enormous – a perfect target. I could sense a million angry eyes were watching me over hidden gun barrels, trigger-fingers tightening. Who would fire first?

We had been prepared for everything – except an invisible enemy, and silence.

Before any hostility arrived, we scrambled off the beach, moving between white tapes the Royal Engineers were already putting down to show where mines had been cleared. Then we set about filming the landings.

On our beach, landing troops tried to dry out in the early sun; then formed up and pressed inland through the fields, interrupted occasionally by Italians who wanted to surrender to somebody – *please!*

Beachmasters were already in control. Tank Landing Craft disgorged enormous self-propelled guns, armoured bulldozers and Sherman tanks. RAF liaison officers talked to their radios. The Navy flagged craft into landing positions. One LST was on a sandbank, another churning the sea and trying to tow it off. Three-ton amphibious DUKWS – great topless trucks that swim – purred purposefully between ships and shore. The first prisoners arrived back on the beach, and wounded were carried into regimental aid posts. Royal Engineers were clearing mines and Pioneers laying wire netting road strips. Military police came ashore and began to control landing traffic. Bofors crews took up defensive positions and dug in. Fresh drinking water was pumped from LST tanks into canvas reservoirs. Petrol, ammunition and food dumps were started. A de-waterproofing area for trucks was marked out. Pioneers started to build and improve tracks and work on Pachino airstrip, which had been well ploughed by the Italians; by midday it was ready for use. All that was what the months of planning had been about.

We filmed the Eighth Army getting set to go places – and so far, to our relief and amazement, few shots had been fired in anger. XIII Corps took a thousand prisoners, that first day. I saw some of our invading troops with tough NCOs actually *marching* smartly up the enemy-held beach in columns of three – not a scene you expect to see on the first day of the re-conquest of Europe. What – no bearskins?

We had been braced to face the fury of the Wehrmacht. In fact, all we faced were a few peasants and goats, and the usual hit-and-run Luftwaffe dive-bombers. It was quite a relaxed way to start an invasion. So far we had on our side most of the military strength and all the surprise, and as the troops came ashore some of our hesitant Italian enemies – local farm workers – waved and smiled. It's always comforting to have the audience on your side.

Towards the evening of D-Day I rounded up a few sergeant-cameramen who had landed nearby with other units and we settled in a field for our first European brew-up. On went the tea in its regulation sooty billycan and the bacon sizzled, supported by our first trophy of war: fat Sicilian tomatoes. A few Messerschmidts came over and did what they could, bombing ships and strafing beaches, but I don't think my new Scottish friends of the 51st Division suffered many casualties. Our surprise had been total.

At dusk, finding our blankets were still somewhere at sea, we settled down on the damp rocky soil of the tomato grove and in an unnatural silence, slept uneasily.

Such lack of enemy opposition was unexpected – and so of course was the hidden fact that, after this first easy day, it was going to take another 665 days to fight our way up the length of Italy, from Pachino to the Swiss frontier by way of Catania, Messina, Salerno, Naples, Anzio, Rome, Florence, through the Gothic Line and out into the Po Valley, to Milan and Venice . . . and victory?

I did not know that I faced 22 months of battle that was going to provide some of the worst experiences of my life – and a few of the best.

THEY ENLISTED THE GODFATHER . . .

The stunning thud of bombs shook us awake. The lurid nightscape was bright as day. We jumped up in alarm, our shadows stretching out before us. The Germans had finally reacted.

Their night bombers were dropping flares and hunting targets. They had plenty. We covered the coastline and were impossible to miss. Attempting to hold them off, thousands of glowing Bofors shells climbed up slowly in lazy arcs through the night sky and into the darkness above the flares. They were pretty enough and encouraged us, but did not seem to worry the Luftwaffe. The invasion fleet and the beaches were bombed all night.

There may be no justice in life, but in battle the percentages go even more out of synch. For instance, my batman-driver Fred Talbot was a regulation cheery Cockney sparrer and peacetime bus driver. We saw a lot of war together, without a cross word.

During the planning for the invasion he had been much relieved to learn that, while I was directing our team and carrying my camera along with the first wave of infantry ashore, when I could reasonably expect to get my head knocked-off . . . there would be no room for him. He would have to stay behind with our loaded jeep and sail across in the relative comfort of a larger, safer transport ship. This would land with some dignity a day or two later, when hopefully the shot 'n' shell would have moved on. It was just his good luck, and he was duly thankful.

However on invasion day my first wave went in, as I said, to mystifying silence. The worst we got was wet. Meanwhile, Driver Talbot's ship, preparing to follow the fleet to Sicily and proceeding through the night at a leisurely pace from Sousse towards Sfax and well behind the armada . . . hit a mine and sank immediately.

Talbot spent some hours in the dark sea before being picked up, and another ten hours in a lifeboat. He was one of the few survivors.

When he caught up with us some days later he was rather rueful about the injustice of it all. I passed a few unnecessary remarks about life sometimes being safer at the sharp end, but understandably Talbot was not amused.

My relief at his return was clouded by the knowledge that our jeep, loaded with everything we possessed, was at the bottom of the Med. Down there in the deep lay the Service Dress and gleaming Sam Browne I had worked so hard to achieve and only worn a few times. Now I had nothing resplendent and should have to attend what I anticipated would be the vibrant social scenes in Rome and Florence in my invasion rig – a bit basic and underdressed for any hospitable Contessa's welcoming party . . . War can be cruel.

Then there was my religiously-kept wartime diary. Had those notes brimming with excitement, dates, facts and figures not become an early casualty of war . . . had that mine not destroyed my tenuous literary patience at a time when life was becoming too busy to sit and think and remember and write . . . had that ship not sunk – you could have suffered a version of this book half-a-century ago!

Strangely, having lost everything *but* my life, I felt curiously light-hearted – free and fast-moving. I would recommend travelling light to any Liberator. You sometimes approach this silly carefree mood when an airline has lost your luggage in some unfamiliar city and suddenly you have nothing to carry, or wear, or worry about.

Talbot and I met only once after the war, late one night going home on the District Line, Inner Circle. He was in good shape and told me he was working in Norwich as a ladies' hairdresser.

Next day, still curiously carefree, I watched General Montgomery and Lord Mountbatten land from their Command ship – the Brass setting foot upon Europe. Our piece of their global war was getting under way and, apart from the bombing, we'd met little opposition – certainly not from the crack Parachute and Panzer Grenadier Divisions we were expecting to attack. We moved inland cautiously.

The Italian defences in our sector seemed admirably sited. Their pillboxes commanded excellent fields of fire, were strongly constructed and most had underground chambers full of ammunition. In main positions were six-inch guns, some made in 1907. All sites were deserted; their crews had melted away.

A handful of small Italian tanks did attempt a few brave sorties but their 37mm guns had no chance against Shermans with 75s and heavy armour.

Fifteen miles from the landing beaches, our first capture on the road north to Syracuse and Catania was Noto, once capital of the region and Sicily's finest baroque town. Thankfully it was absolutely untouched by war, and bisected by one tree-lined avenue which climbed from the plain up towards the town square and down the other side. We did not know whether this approach had been cleared of enemy and mines, so advanced carefully.

The population emerged equally cautiously, and lined the road. Then they started, hesitantly, to *clap* – a ripple of applause that followed us into their town.

You clap if you're approving, without being enthusiastic. Nobody cheered – the welcome was restrained. We were not kissed once – nothing so abandoned. It seemed they didn't quite know how to handle being conquered.

Like almost every other village and town we were to reach, Noto's old walls were covered with Fascist slogans. *Credere! Obbedire! Combattere!* – Believe! Obey! Fight! – was popular, though few of the locals seemed to have got its message. Another which never ceased to irritate me was *Il Duce ha sempre ragione* – The Leader is always right! Shades of Big Brother to come. Hard to think of a less-accurate statement; we were in Sicily to point out the error in *that* argument.

Another even less-imaginative piece of propaganda graffiti was just 'DUCE', painted on all visible surfaces. As a hill town came in to focus every wall facing the road would be covered with Duces. Such scattergun publicity was a propaganda tribute to Mussolini, the Dictator who by then had already become the victim of his own impotent fantasies. To me he always appeared more a clown than a threat. To his prisoners he was no joke.

In Noto the baroque Town Hall and Cathedral faced each other, giving us a taste of what war-in-Italy was to become: it would be like fighting through a museum.

We filmed one small unexpected ceremony with a carabinieri officer who had discovered a copy of a 1940 speech to the Italians by Churchill. From the steps of the Casa del Fascio he read it out with many a verbal flourish; an intent audience nodded thoughtfully. Churchill had been promoted from ogre to statesman overnight.

Then three British officers arrived and marched up to the town's War Memorial, where after a respectful silence they gave a formal salute to the commemorated townsfolk who had fallen as our Allies in the Great War. That sensitive and sensible gesture went down *very* well, and for the first time the applause was real. You could see the Sicilians thinking, 'Maybe they're going to be all right, after all!'

Observing both sides in action, I had by now seen enough of the war and the military to appreciate that if you had to be in the army, a film unit was the place to be. It offered as much excitement as you could handle – in some cases, rather more – but also a degree of independence, and even an unmilitary acknowledgement which cut through rank.

We're all susceptible to cameras, though we may pretend to be disinterested and impatient. (Surely you don't want to take *my* picture?) In truth, everyone from General Montgomery down was delighted to be photographed. I spent some time with him during the war and always, as soon as he saw me, he'd start pointing at nothing in particular, but in a most commanding manner. It was his way and it seemed to work; half-a-century ago he had television-style fame, before television.

People do straighten up and pull-in their stomachs when a camera appears. It's an instant reflex – like beauty queens, for instance. As soon as they see a camera, they smile and wave.

Senior army officers were certainly not given to waving but, not quite understanding what we were doing, tended to approach us with impatient exasperation or amused confusion. Usually when they saw we were quite professional they would submit to direction or just leave us alone – which for a junior officer, was ideal.

We drove north and found the 7th Green Howards had captured a large Italian coastal defence position of 12-inch gun-howitzers which could throw a 610lb shell 20 miles. They were pointing towards our carefree arrival route and positioned to do terrible damage to any invader, but were only as good as their crews – who fortunately were not working that day.

We noticed with some bitterness towards international Arms Kings that they had been manufactured by British Vickers-Armstrong. Our 74th Field Regiment got them firing on German positions outside Catania, the biggest guns the Eighth Army had ever operated – so I suppose it worked out all right in the end.

Another capture worked out equally well, and Sergeant S.A. Gladstone got some expressive pictures of happy troops liberating cellars containing 7,000 gallons of good red wine. As trophies go, this was vintage and generally accepted as even better booty than tomatoes.

After our carefree advance from the beach, resistance had toughened in front of the Eighth Army. German paratroops had been flown in from France and the Hermann Goering Division replaced the timid and apathetic Italians. After tough fighting on the beaches, the Americans enjoyed an easier run through east and central Sicily, then followed the Germans around the giant sentinel of Mount Etna as they pulled back and prepared to retreat to the mainland.

As for our enemies, we soon discovered that the Italians in their rickety little tanks were anxious to become our prisoners, and the Germans in their enormous 57-ton Tiger tanks were anxious to kill us – so at least we knew where we were . . .

Sergeant Radford and I set off across the island to be in at the capture of Palermo by General Patton's army. That pugnacious American General had just been in deep trouble after visiting a hospital where he slapped and abused two privates he believed were malingering. The soldiers were said to be suffering, like the rest of us, from 'battle fatigue'. They had no wounds though one was found to have mild dysentery, yet they seriously affected the war. Patton's exasperation was demonstrated in front of an accompanying War Correspondent, and the resultant Stateside publicity put the General's career on hold for a year – and in due course provided a tragic death-knell for Churchill's Anzio campaign, which needed Patton's drive and leadership.

As we drove through remote and untouched mountain villages, we were the first Allied soldiers they had seen. Wine was pressed upon us and haircuts (including a friction) cost a couple of cigarettes. Even the almost unsmokable 'V' cigarettes made for the Eighth Army in India were eagerly bartered.

In Palermo householders peeped timidly around their curtains, wondering whether our dust-covered khaki was field-grey? The city was peaceful – blue trams were running and the police with swords and tricornes drifted about, as well dressed as Napoleonic officers.

After an RAF visit, the harbour was full of half-sunken gunboats, each surrounded by shoals of large fish. We caught a few by hitting them with stones. Izaac Walton must have been spinning.

Posters showed a monstrous John Bull, the world his rounded stomach as he swallowed more lands. Another was of a grinning skeleton in a British steel helmet. I took pictures of them while passers-by hurried on, fearful lest I turn and blame them.

We returned across Sicily to the Eighth Army HQ on the malarial Lentini plain – indeed a large number of our casualties were from mosquitoes. During the night we felt huge shuddering explosions outside Catania and watched sheets of flame light the sky. The Germans were blowing-up their ammunition dumps – so they were about to start their escape to the mainland.

A new officer had arrived to join us: Lieutenant A.Q. McLaren who, captured in the desert by Rommel's Afrika Korps while using two cameras, had refused to hand one over because it was personal property and demanded a receipt for the War Office Ikonta. He later escaped, still carrying the receipt.

As we were meeting, an operational message came in saying that Catania was about to fall. We scrambled off to get the pictures. McLaren was driving ahead of me, standing up in the cab of his truck watching for enemy aircraft, as we all had to. This gave a few seconds' warning if the Luftwaffe swooped down to strafe the road.

We drove in column around the diversion at reeking Dead Horse Corner. In the dust ahead lay a German mine. McLaren's warning scream came too late. It was his first day in Sicily.

The patient infantry plodding past us moved on silently towards the city. They had seen another violent death and perhaps they too would soon stop a bullet or a shellburst. In an hour or so some of them would also be dead, and they knew it.

The whole direction of their lives now was to reach some unknown place and, if possible, kill any unknown Germans they found there. In battle, death is always present and usually unemotional, and when it approaches, inches can mean the march goes on – or you are still and resting, for ever.

However its proximity does wipe away life's other problems. Those plodding figures passing Dead Horse Corner and McLaren's body were not worrying about unpaid bills or promotion or nagging wives or even sergeant majors. Getting through the day alive was achievement enough.

It took the population of Catania some time to realise that the Germans had gone. Then they came out into the streets to cheer and show their relief, carrying flowers, fruit, wine ... It was hard to see them as enemies. Our pictures showed Italian nurses tending the wounded of the Durham Light Infantry.

At this point Sergeants Herbert and Travis arrived and unintentionally captured Catania's entire police force. This was not in the shot-list. They had left their jeep behind a blown bridge on the road into town and were filming on foot when a civilian car came out of the city towards them. Surprised by such an apparition in a war zone, they commandeered it and ordered the driver to turn round and take them into Catania.

Speeding ahead of the Army, he whizzed excitedly along back streets and finally through two huge gates into a palace courtyard full of armed carabinieri. As the gates slammed behind them and they looked around at massed uniforms ... suspicion dawned that now *they* might be the prisoners.

Then the Commandant in an elegant uniform arrived, saluted, and asked for their orders. That was better. They ventured that they were just a couple of photographers who did not really want a police force, not just then. However, they did want transport.

They were instantly ushered into a large garage crammed with every type of vehicle, their choice was filled with petrol and the ignition key presented with a flourish. Amid salutes, the conquering sergeants drove out through the massive gates, at speed. Honour had been satisfied on all sides.

The object of much planning-ahead during the final fighting through Sicily was not the capture of Messina, straddling the enemy's escape route and well-protected by Kesselring's massed anti-aircraft guns, but of Taormina, an hour's drive to its south. This charming honeymoon-village of the Twenties climbs the rocky coast in the shadow of Mount Etna's 11,000 feet. Like Capri, its flowers, pretty villas and bright social life gave it a sort of Noël Coward appeal. It was untouched by war, of course, as all armies protect places they might wish to use as headquarters, or billets.

It was a placid scene, as we arrived. Out in the bay a British gunboat lay peacefully at anchor, while a number of anxious Italian soldiers were standing on the beach trying to surrender to it. They would probably have been almost as satisfied if anyone else had paused to capture them – even a passing Film Unit – but by this time we had all become rather blasé about Italian prisoners. They had lost their scarcity value.

My CO Geoffrey Keating and our War Artist friend Edward Ardizzone had reached Taormina ahead of the army patrols. I was surprised poor old Ted could climb the mountainside because he seemed to be overweight and getting on a bit – he was at least 40. However he struggled up the 800 feet from the seashore – not as elegantly as Noël arriving at the beginning of Act 2 but in time for them to requisition, breathlessly, the Casa Cuseni. This splendid little villa built of golden stone was owned before the war by an expatriate British artist. Its garden was heady with the exotic scent of orange blossom, its library equally heady with pornography.

Despite those distractions, the defeat of the Germans in Sicily meant that we at last had time to be happy, even as we prepared for the coming invasion of the mainland. Every evening we relaxed with a Sicilian white in the hush of the garden terrace as the sun set behind Mount Etna. This was war at its best . . .

The 10,000 square miles of Sicily had been captured in 38 days, during which the Allies suffered 31,158 casualties. The Wehrmacht had lost 37,000 men, the Italians 130,000 – most of them, of course, prisoners getting out of the war alive.

In its successful strategic withdrawal, the German army corps had little air and no naval support, yet its 60,000 men stood up to two Allied armies of 450,000 men – and finally some 55,000 of them escaped across the Straits of Messina to Italy to fight another day. They took with them 10,000 vehicles and 50 tanks. Generalfeldmarschall Kesselring – the troops called him 'Laughing Albert' – had enough to laugh about at this Dunkirk victory.

Our last pictures of the Sicilian campaign showed Generals Eisenhower and Montgomery staring symbolically through field glasses out across the Straits of Messina towards the toe of Italy, and the enemy. That was to be our next step towards the end of the war. Behind them in Sicily, an Allied military government was being established, though in fact control of the island was falling back through the years into the hands of the island's secret army – the Mafia.

Our victory was darkened by the fact that behind the scenes – and with the very *best* of intentions, you understand – the Americans were handing Sicily back to its former masters. In a misguided military decision, they enlisted the Godfather!

From his prison cell in New York State, Lucky Luciano, then *Capo di tutti Capi*, arranged Mafia support and guidance for the Allies in Sicily – in return of course for various business concessions. So it was that Lucky was released from prison and flown-back to his homeland to 'facilitate the invasion' – and on the side, to set-up the Mafia's new narcotics empire. Vito Genovese, well-known New York hoodlum wanted for murder and various crimes in America, turned up in uniform in Sicily as a liaison officer attached to the US Army. Through threats and graft and skill, their contingent soon out-manoeuvred our unworldly do-gooding AMGOT, the Allied Military Government of Occupied Territory. We had our card marked by gangsters.

Thus the victors helped destroy Mussolini's rare achievement; he had held the Mafia down and all-but destroyed its power. Now in their rush to pacify an island already peaceful, the Americans resuscitated another convicted Mafiosi, Don Calò Vizzini, and put him in control of the island's civil Administration with military vehicles and supplies at his disposal. The Mafia was born again, fully grown.

Since then even Italian Prime Ministers have been found to enjoy such connections and support. For example, the 113-mile Palermo to Messina autostrada was finally inaugurated after 35 years by Silvio Berlusconi in December 2004. It cost £500 million and was partly funded by Brussels and the European Investment Bank. Work had begun in 1969 and, following the regular siphoning-off of materials and funds by the Mafia, proceeded at a rate of three miles a *year*.

Fortunately for our lively sense of mission, we simple soldiers in our shining armour knew nothing of the Mafia's rebirth, nor could we foresee it. We had no time to occupy ourselves with the future crime and corruption that was to inherit our victory. We were busy fighting a war and preparing for an attack on Italy's mainland.

So the Allies left five million Sicilians to a future often controlled by the Mafia, and a resigned tourist industry which in the peacetime-to-come would advertise: 'Invade Sicily – everyone *else* has . . .'

At the end of August, the only Germans left in Sicily were the 7,000 ruminating behind barbed wire. General Montgomery's headquarters in the San Domenico, former convent and now the grandest hotel in Taormina, prepared for the first visit of the Allied Commander of the Mediterranean Theatre, General

Dwight D. Eisenhower, then almost unknown outside the US – and little-known within it.

An American Supreme Commander with all those stars was something quite new to us, so he was accorded the full military razzle-dazzle and then some, as only the British Army knows how to lay on.

He had flown into Catania with a sparkle of five American Generals and a fighter escort. They drove up the coast road to Taormina. The Highland Division – the men with whom I had invaded Sicily – were now *much* better-dressed and pressed, and turned out their most impressive Parade of Honour: pipe band, swirling kilts, white blanco, stamping feet, loads of swank ... They marched about, then crashed to attention and Presented Arms. We waited for the Commander-in-Chief's soldierly appraisal. 'Say' he said at last, 'some swell outfit.'

It seemed a fair comment.

I STILL FEEL RATHER GUILTY
ABOUT THAT . . .

During our serene sessions on the terrace of the Casa Cuseni we even had time to take silly shots for home consumption of ourselves larking about – 'red-hots', we called them.

I can't remember the reason for such warriors' relaxation. The photographs were taken in the morning, so demon vino was no excuse. Why then do grown men behave in such a way? I think we should be told.

I suspect dear old Alfred Black may have instigated the pictorial fooling around; son of George Black, the impresario who ran the Palladium and other theatres in London and Blackpool, he probably directed our light-hearted romps. The pictures were taken, I suspect, for the lovely Roma Beaumont, one of Ivor Novello's leading ladies from *The Dancing Years* and such, who was also Alf's wife. This was the only occasion I can recall during the war when we had the time or the taste for jolly frolics.

More seriously, we considered future picture-coverage of the war on the Italian mainland, which was going to mean splitting our Unit. First it had to be decided whether Captain Harry Rignold or I should lead our cameramen across the Straits at

Réggio Calabria to cover the Eighth Army's opening assault upon Italy.

The other would return to Africa to join the more militarily significant operation *Buttress,* the landing a week later up the coast near Salerno by the new and American-controlled Fifth Army. That bay, thirty-five miles south of Naples, was at the extreme limit of our vital air cover.

Rignold, my senior, had the choice of course. We had spent some days together driving and filming through central Sicily, and I had come to like and much admire him. Small and soft-spoken, he was a most unmilitary figure, but brave and eager. He had caught the excitement of an assault landing while filming at Narvik in Norway, May 1940. That landing was a combined operation and, like Dieppe, a considerable defeat – but for Harry a splendid photo opportunity. So he chose Salerno, the bigger story – and was killed on the beach. I went across the Straits of Messina with the 2nd Inniskilling Fusiliers – the ferocious 'Skins' – and landed safely. I had drawn another lucky card.

Taormina had been too good to last. Very soon we were reminded there was a war to be won, and our serenity each twilight had been a sort of mirage.

So we dispersed and set off to fight once again. Harry Rignold left for Africa with his cameramen, and on the evening of September 3 '43 my sergeants and I boarded our LCIs in Catania docks. We were back at war as a sort of decoy invasion, hoping to lure German divisions down south and away from the coming Salerno landing.

As we settled in, the massed invasion fleet due to sail that night was attacked by German fighter-bombers. So much, we thought, for surprise. They already had the *un*welcome mat out . . .

On the fourth anniversary of Britain's entry into the war we sailed from the comforting shores of Sicily, where by now we felt we were at home among friends. The fleet assembled off the coast, and at dawn our silent armada approached the dark mountains and narrow beaches of Italy's toe.

The Straits of Messina are less than three miles wide. Should we get into any trouble, I felt we could swim across, backwards or forwards. We were to land along a five-mile stretch of beach north of Réggio. It reminded me of our invasion of Sicily, but through a golden mist across a smoother sea. Already I was feeling like an assured veteran: been there, invaded that . . .

During our peaceful days in Taormina the Royal Artillery had drawn up all its biggest guns around Messina and now set about pinpointing and silencing any enemy batteries across the Straits.

As we neared our landing beach the massed gunners behind us used up the Royal Artillery's Sicilian reserves of ammunition, supported by the rocket-firing devil-ships which were sailing alongside us. These were landing craft packed with launchers firing 800 five-inch rockets in 30 seconds. Each contained 30lb of TNT. They tore open the sky with an insane howling madness that filled all men – friends and foe – with shock and fear.

There was no reply from the enemy artillery – and it was easy to understand why! Some shells crashed around us into the sea. They were ours, falling short – but even so, were not welcome. Friendly fire can hurt just as much. Still no answer from the enemy coast.

At 5.30am we hit the beach and ran inland to escape any German fire. It did not arrive. The Luftwaffe flew in to strafe and bomb, but otherwise the Eighth Army once again walked ashore almost unopposed. It seemed in the last few days the Wehrmacht had withdrawn to man its next defensive line across Italy – or perhaps had picked-up warning Intelligence about the coming landing at Salerno. We had fired 400 tons of HE at empty hillsides.

Encouraged by the absence of resistance, Driver Talbot and I set off to chase the enemy inland – but cautiously. We drove past huge Italian coastal guns near Pellaro, also made by Vickers in 1930, also unmanned. It was like a holiday drive, through lovely scenery.

Then, rounding a bend in the mountain road, we were confronted by an approaching column of a couple of hundred Italian soldiers bound for the invasion beach, all belligerently armed and evidently ready to resist our attack upon their homeland.

As Talbot froze in horror, it dawned upon me that my .38 Smith and Wesson revolver – our only armament – was still beneath my reissued kit at the bottom of my new kitbag. My old kitbag was still at the bottom of the Med. I was not a fearsome figure.

In that instant I realised, with regret, that I had been thinking too much about pictures when war is for fighting. In a film unit preoccupied with observation, it was all too easy to fall into the role of detached spectator – you can't shoot me, Jerry, I'm just watching – when everyone else has taken sides and is trying to kill you.

At OCTU back in Barmouth I had absorbed the military dictum that Attack is the Best Form of Defence, so I leapt smartly from the jeep, using strong language and brandishing my camera. It was, at that moment, all I *had* to brandish.

To my surprise it was most effective. No one shot me – indeed, the massed Italians were delighted. Guns were put down, combs appeared, buttons done up, and the whole troop gathered around me manoeuvring for position, flashing eager smiles and showing their best sides for the picture. Look at me, Ma, I'm surrendering!

They were all going home, they told me, for the war was over between our nations and peace had been declared. This was quite inaccurate but at 200 to 2, I was not about to argue. Anything that made them happy was all right by me. I took loads of pictures and warmly commended them to our nearest fighting unit just a few miles down the road, regretting that I was unable to accept prisoners – or even co-belligerents – however amiable. In my experience this is *not* a ploy that works with the German Army.

During the whole jolly surrender I was earnestly hoping that the successful and invasion-happy Eighth Army would not suddenly come bursting around the corner in our footsteps, all guns blazing. Fortunately it was too far behind.

We parted with mutual expressions of relief and regard. Their eager surrender to the following infantry was, unfortunately, a little premature. Italy did not capitulate for another five days during which they all went, not home but towards the start of a journey to a POW camp in Africa, as its final prisoners.

They didn't even get their prints. I still feel rather guilty about that . . .

VERY BAD JOKES INDEED . . .

After our peaceful, almost gentlemanly invasion of Réggio Calabria, the Eighth Army advanced 100 miles in five days. It was the only week in the whole Italian campaign that could be described as Easy. Afterwards the Germans, the terrain and the weather combined against us.

Hoping not to attract any more would-be prisoners, Talbot and I drove north up the big toe of Italy. Just past the coastal bunion at Vibo Valéntia, we took over a house in the small town of Nicastro – and there made a new friend.

He was a small brown mongrel with large appealing eyes who instantly grew accustomed to our faces, and our army rations. By the time we were ready to move on towards Cosenza, we had become inseparable and he was part of AFPU, keeping an eye on things. He rode between us in the jeep, bright and alert, answering to his new and natural name: Nic. Pleasant to have a dog about the place – makes you feel more like a family.

We three set out one bright clear morning, planning to go as far north as we could, until the Germans reacted. After an hour or so we picked a sunny spot for lunch, and lay around enjoying the calm and the scenery. Then suddenly across the valley behind us we saw a familiar threatening scene approaching, fast: a convoy of RASC trucks following our road to the front and throwing up the usual dense dust-clouds.

This was the torment of all unsurfaced country roads in summer. Find yourself off-tarmac and amid traffic and within minutes your jeep and you would be a living statue, thick-coated by a pea-souper of choking dust.

Panic! We had to get away before the convoy arrived or we should be eating their dust and driving slowly through their clouds for hours.

We slung the remains of our picnic into the back of the jeep, along with ration boxes and everything we had unloaded for the siesta. We got moving as the first truck rounded the nearby bend, trailing its white cloud and heading implacably towards us. I gunned the jeep and we sailed away, just in front of the choking clouds. *Phew.*

We easily out-ran the convoy and were alert also to the survival warning of the Army's inescapable sign: Dust Brings Shells. It must have been an hour later when I was hunting through the disordered jeep for my maps when we suddenly remembered . . . Where's *Nic?*

In the frenzy to get away through clear air, we had left the poor little chap finishing his lunch . . . and about to be engulfed in a maelstrom of trucks and noise and dust.

We waited for the convoy to pass, then for their dust to settle, then drove back to hunt around our picnic location, calling his name. No echo of that cheerful bark. No wagging tail, no excited recognition. Perhaps he had struck off across country towards Nicastro for the unexpired portion of his day's rations? Perhaps he had been picked up by someone in that convoy? Stricken, we never risked our affections again. Goodbye Nic, young Italian charmer lost in action.

Heading on through the mountains, we paused to relieve an internment camp, full of civilians of various nationalities. You would think detainees who had been imprisoned for many months would have been delighted to see Allies in liberating-mode, riding to their rescue? Not a bit of it.

Their guards had run away, and now some 50 of Mussolini's prisoners, having raided the camp kitchen, were enjoying a family picnic under the trees. They were a well-dressed group lazing around in a scene of contentment.

Then some of the younger male detainees took me aside and mentioned that by freeing them I was not doing them any favours: they'd had a cushy billet with regular meals and no worries, living a peaceful country life with other friendly families, many of whom had pretty young daughters. They were quite content to escape wartime worries outside the wire, with nothing to do all day except lie around in the long grass and be charming. Furthermore, their sex lives had *never* been so good.

Unamused, I offered to lock them up again and throw away the key. On reflection they reluctantly decided to accept the worrisome freedom I had thrust upon them. Their cheerful group did contrive to make my war seem rather pointless.

I left them to their bucolic pursuits and got back on the road north, chasing reality. This soon became all too apparent when on the west coast of Italy three Allied Divisions of the Fifth Army steamed in from Africa and attempted a landing near Salerno – to face the most savage resistance of the war, led by the 16th Panzer Division.

Another easy landing had been expected after the dismissal of Mussolini and Italy's surrender, but this was no longer the musical-comedy *bella figura* battle – just going through the motions – that the Italians had undertaken without the equipment or the will to fight. These were fierce and determined counter-attacks by crack German divisions which had been expecting – even rehearsing for – our landing. The Fifth Army, exposed and vulnerable, seemed about to be destroyed before even gaining a toehold on Italy.

AFPU had four officers and eleven sergeant-cameramen covering this different sort of assault landing. As they sailed in, one landing craft was hit by 20 enemy shells. Others exploded as they struck mines or were strafed by the Luftwaffe squadrons which were out in strength. In the chaos some craft put in to wrong beaches. The precise invasion timetable disintegrated.

Sergeant R.P. Lambert, our smallest photographer, was in an LCI heading for the beach, standing behind a tall infantryman of the Queen's Regiment. The tense silence was broken when a soldier leaned down and whispered, 'If that guy steps into the sea and disappears, Sarge, *you* ain't half gonna get wet.'

Such a cheery routine exactly followed those morale-boosting war movies. From officers came similar flip Ealing comedy throwaways about seeing Naples and dying. These soon proved to be very bad jokes indeed.

Harry Rignold, my opposite number, had landed from an LCI and was moving across the beach when a shell burst in the sand in front of his jeep. His right hand was blown off. Sergeant Penman and their driver were also injured.

Harry walked calmly to the sea wall, carrying his camera in his remaining hand. Putting it down carefully he said, 'I'm going to the RAP to get my arm fixed.'

He was lying on a stretcher at the regimental aid post awaiting evacuation by ship when another shell fell amid the wounded and killed that gentle and excellent man. He died without knowing he had been awarded the Military Cross.

Above: The Italians' coastal defence guns (made in Britain) could have done our invasion great damage – had they been manned by grown-ups . . .

Above: General Montgomery landed in Reggio in an amphibious DUKW instead of his usual Humber, to be greeted by pipers of the 51st Highland Division.

Above: When he saw a camera Monty would always point at something, in a most commanding way.

Right: I went with him for his first meeting with General Mark Clark, whose Fifth Army had landed behind enemy lines. The beleaguered Clark welcomes Monty to his Beachhead.

Above: Monty goes to explain to Clark and his Chief-of-Staff Major General Gruenther how the Eighth Army will help the Fifth. (His Officer-in-Attendance is the regulation two paces behind).

Below: The Americans did not receive the usual Liberation-welcome in Naples, where the population was still stunned by bombing and German destruction.

Above: My opposite number in AFPU, the brave and gentle Captain Harry Rignold, was killed during the landing on Salerno beach.

Above: For months the German positions holding up our advance around Monte Cassino resisted all Allied attacks . . .

Left: . . . despite powerful support by artillery, from 4.2" mortars, and up . . .

Above: . . . and by Sherman
Tanks . . .

Right: . . . so finally 239
Flying Fortresses flew in
to destroy the Benedictine
Monastery which had stood
amid the wild peaks of the
Abruzzi for 1,400 years.

Above: Some of the 453½ tons of bombs that fell on Cassino in the first aerial attack.

Below: The ancient citadel of art and learning, after the bombing.

Left: After our triumphant assault landing at Anzio, *this* was as close to Rome as we got for almost five months: the Flyover. Later, when the Germans launched three major attacks to throw us back into the sea, this was as far as *they* got.

Right: Infantrymen under attack in the wadis. Even a small ditch seemed secure and reassuring.

Below: A German view of the battle, as they occupied their side of the Flyover.

Above: On the road to Rome an Italian cyclist voices his opinion of the German Army – by then safely disarmed and marching to the stockade.

Right: Taking pictures in a POW camp, one face seemed to me to symbolize the end of Teutonic dreams of conquest. I called this portrait 'The Master Race'. Next to that tragic figure, a young German POW appreciated that, for him at least, the war was over.

Along the beach Sergeant J. Huggett ha
Ahead of him some Commandos were ho
tory against heavy German counter-attac
game, set off up the hill to get pictures of
top an angry voice ordered, 'This way! `
Commando officer.

'You took your bloody time, Sergeant,'
the hell are your men?' Huggett admitted
alone, to get pictures. '*What?*' cried the of
tional silence, 'I called for reinforcemen
photographer.'

One understands exactly how he felt; there
you just don't want your picture taken – even th
be your last . . .

The Luftwaffe flew in close-support for K
sions; for the first time we were outnumber
desperately. After two days the landing was
the Allied Commander, the American Gene
pared plans for re-embarkation. He seeme
and go home. His Army had only one esca
was unnerving to learn that our own Co
considered running back to the ships and sai

He was eventually discouraged by tou
senior American and British officers like
Troubridge who could see that an attempt
beaches dominated by German artillery in
would be a massacre. They bullied and
against the possibility of retreat, but for in
faced their first major defeat.

The crisis on the beaches followed
drawn up by inexperienced officers in
assault divisions had been given defensi

the
too
batt
coo
our
des

nir
ne
of
se

Sa
to
rea
cry
45t
tea
bitt
this

G
evac
Maj
beac
It
Com
still,
Serv
Li
grad
was
the w

6th Division, carried the lone offensive role – but was landed
ar from Salerno for its execution. The result was a desperate
e to establish the beachhead by three separate and un-
erating forces. There was also a seven-mile gap between
X Corps and the US VI Corps. No wonder General Clark
aired.

ack at AFHQ Eisenhower had heard that his friend was plan-
re-embarkation, and worried that he might have lost his
e. He told his USN ADC that Clark should show the spirit
naval Captain and if necessary, go down with his ship. This
ned unlikely.

ne echo of the desperation on the beaches survives in
rno today: in a tidy but little-visited monumental garden in
stands a very small memorial. You need to crouch down to
its inscription. Few passers-by would notice its anguished
– the thoughts and reactions of the men of the American
Infantry Division which put ashore two regimental combat
s under Major General Troy Middleton. Their scorn and
rness is conveyed by two quotations inscribed on this stone,
memory of desperation.

neral Mark Clark US Fifth Army Commander: '*Prepare to
ate the beach.*' Underneath, the words of his subordinate,
r General Middleton: '*Leave the water and the ammo on the
The 45th Division is here to stay.*'

s rare indeed for a division to castigate publicly its Army
mander for considering sailing away from the battle. Rarer
President Roosevelt later awarded Clark the Distinguished
e Cross for gallantry at Salerno.

utenant General Mark W. Clark – Wayne to his friends –
ated from West Point in 1917, 109th in a class of 135, and
terwards a Captain for 16 years. His career took-off with
r and the friendship of General Eisenhower, with whom he

Left: An enemy 15cm
armoured Infantry
Howitzer in firing
position amid the ruins
of Carroceto.

Below: Captured
American troops are
marched through Rome,
under armed guard.

Right: Other German
soldiers are less
dominant. Held at
gunpoint after capture
by New Zealand troops
during the Battle
of Cassino.

shared an apartment in London. At 46 he became the youngest Lieutenant General the US Army had ever known, with a passion for publicity already well established. As Fifth Army Commander in Italy he refused to stay in the Royal Palace in Naples, explaining humbly to the Press that he felt lost in a big city. He had been raised in Chicago.

Caserta, 30 miles to the north, was the Allied forces headquarters during the war. This enormous mid-18th century palace had been built by the Bourbon King Charles IV to outdo Versailles, but General Clark still found no suitable accommodation within its 1200 rooms, so set up a trailer, a converted truck, in the formal gardens behind the Palace – which as he explained in resultant publicity, was no place for an American cowboy.

The fate of the Salerno landing hung in the balance for some two weeks. A major factor in the outcome was the supporting firepower of the big naval cruisers offshore, and the dropping into the Beachhead on two successive nights of two regimental combat teams from the tough US 82nd Airborne Division. This operation, though sadly delayed, was probably the most successful airborne operation of the war, and swung the battle.

At a time when most things were going wrong, the British army faced that most unusual and wretched event: a mutiny, in which British NCOs were sentenced to death.

Some 700 reinforcement troops had arrived by LST from Naples. They sat down on the beach and refused to report to their new units. All were desert veterans of the 50th Northumbrian and 51st Highland Division who had learned they were going straight back into the line to fight – and not with old comrades and officers they respected, but with new divisions. Worse, some Scots were going to non-Scottish regiments. They all believed they had been promised home rotation with their original units.

It was not until the Commander of X Corps, the popular Lieutenant General Richard McCreery, went to the beach that the majority were persuaded to obey orders, though 192 still refused and were later court-martialled. The NCOs who led the rebellion were sentenced to death, but were soon given the chance to redeem themselves by returning to duty in Italy, with suspended sentences. They did not suffer the ultimate penalty. However, the Salerno mutiny remained a permanent stain on the honour of the Army, and is not mentioned in the Official War History.

All this time I was with the Eighth Army as it moved up the Calabrian toe of Italy. There were two coastal roads, both so narrow there was little room for the two divisions in action – the 5th up the west coast, the 1st Canadian to the east. Only one brigade at a time – sometimes one battalion – could get into the front line of the toe, to fight. It was a geographical gift for German demolition experts; one blown bridge could hold up an army for as long as its ruins could be defended.

After facing the 16th Panzer Division north of Termoli, the Eighth captured the vital Foggia airfield complex, which opened-up southern Europe to Allied bombers and allowed close air support within minutes. At the River Sangro, General Montgomery issued another of his calls to action which always sounded to me like an invitation to cricket: 'We will now deal the enemy a colossal whack . . .' It was his last battle before he returned to England to prepare for the Second Front.

Some Russian officers under General Vasiliev were visiting the Front and, surprisingly, were familiar with Monty's terminology, but old Eighth Army hands were unprepared for Major General Solodovnic. He had last been seen in Africa in the more casual uniform of a War Correspondent reporting for the TASS news agency. He was not bemused by Monty's sporting appeals – indeed had a habit of putting haughty Brigade Majors on the defensive: 'I suppose you're one of the Upper Classes?'

On September 8 '43, the day before the Salerno landing, Italy had capitulated and become a co-belligerent, ostensibly on our side. The conquest of Sicily had knocked Mussolini off his perch, and Italy out of the war. Having as a neutral enjoyed the flattering attentions of both sides, the Duce had delayed his declaration of war too long to claim any significant share of Hitler's blitzkrieg spoils. The Germans overran France so quickly, the Italians contributed so little – and Mussolini had waited 280 days, until June 10 '40, before declaring war. He could make few appeals at the armistice table. His demand for Nice, Tunis and Corsica received little sympathy from Hitler, who had once complained bitterly: 'The Italians never lose a war. No matter what happens, they *always* end up on the winning side.' He was right again – but the chastened Mussolini saw it another way: 'Nobody likes a neutral.'

After the surrender of Sicily the Italian King and Government had been anxious to get rid of their Duce. He was eager to show it was not his fault that Fascism and much of Sicily were in ruins, with more to come. In an attempt to avoid the war spreading north through Italy, the diminutive King Victor Emmanuel III – who had brought Mussolini to power in 1922 – belatedly demanded his resignation and replaced him by Marshal Badoglio. After that bloodless coup the Duce, more confused than angry, accepted his dismissal, and they parted amicably.

A few months later he was rescued from house arrest at Gran Sasso on the highest peak of the Apennines by glider-borne paratroops led by Hitler's personal commando, Colonel Otto Skorzeny. Mussolini was then reinstated by the Führer for a brief spell in the twilight zone of doomed Dictators.

Negotiating a change of sides for Italy during the war had been trickier than surrendering. A secret armistice negotiated by the captured British General Carton de Wiart had been signed, but the Italian Field Command was not informed. It did not know what to do so ended up, in the Italian way, by doing nothing.

Unfortunately at that moment Allied command was also indecisive and at Salerno, almost overwhelmed. Instead of ordering the Italian Army to turn and fight the Germans as planned and dropping a division of paratroops on Rome Airport, the Allies threw up their hands, ignored the new situation, cancelled the airdrop – and continued slogging up Italy as though nothing had happened.

For weeks the Germans had been expecting their ally to defect, so with their usual fast reaction seized Rome and rounded up the 600,000 obedient Italian soldiers who had remained in their camps and not gone home and changed into civvies. Instead, they went into cattle trucks and off to German labour camps.

Curiously, Whitehall now reacted in an Italianate way. When their prison camp guards packed up and went home most British POWs had planned to scatter and take to the mountains, but a War Office Brigadier, a Deputy Director of Military Intelligence, ordered them *not* to break-out of their camps. So within 48 hours half the British POWs in Italy also found themselves under German guard and on their way to prison camps in Germany.

The only decisive action in the whole theatre was taken by Vesuvius, which erupted for the first time in 38 years and then grumbled on for weeks under giant incandescent candles and angry plumes of fire and rock. The naval Commander-in-Chief issued an admiring statement: 'The Naples group of ports is now discharging at a rate of 12 million tons a year. Vesuvius is estimated to be doing 30 million tons a *day*. We cannot but admire this gesture of the Gods.'

Suddenly I received a gesture from a military god: I was ordered to drive urgently through the mountains to the west coast and go to a small beach south of Salerno. Purpose and location: top secret. There I boarded a waiting torpedo boat, rakish and sinister. It was there to carry General Montgomery to his first meeting with the beleaguered General Mark Clark, behind enemy lines and on the other side of the Salerno beachhead. It was just the two of us, at sea with a Royal Navy crew from Malta.

We set off flat-out, engines roaring, in a big arc around the enemy-held coast, watching for German E-boats which I was told we could *probably* out-run. I was comforted by my belief that nobody was going to risk the life of Britain's only victorious General, without a *very* good reason.

After four hours pounding through a calm sea without sighting another craft we came in to shore, transferred to a waiting DUKW – and there on the beach was Mark Clark, tall and gaunt, with Major General Gruenther and his staff. 'Mighty pleased to see you, General,' he told Monty – and as Fifth Army seemed about to be thrown back into the sea, we could believe he meant it.

His headquarter tents were alongside a rough airstrip hacked out of the scrub where fighters continually took-off and landed. Signs by the road said: 'Aircraft Have Right Of Way.'

After his discussion with General Clark for a couple of hours, General Montgomery and I returned to our torpedo boat to race south for another four hours, hoping the E-boats had not yet been alerted.

Helping the Fifth Army to get established on shore and out of trouble, was to be General Montgomery's Italian swansong before he left to prepare for the Second Front in Normandy.

I sat with him as we bounced through the Tyrrhenian Sea, hoping we were unheard and invisible. In fact this ultimate torpedo boat had a resonant roar that filled the dark sky, and a churning wash that fell back, pounding, towards the horizon. It seemed determined to advertise its presence.

As we ate 'the unexpired portion of the day's ration' I began to appreciate how American senior officers with little or no battle experience found Monty impossible. He always knew he was right – and indeed he usually *was*, though diplomacy and tact were virtues with which he was unfamiliar. He did not work with people, he told them what to do. He was fond of his boss Field Marshal Alexander, but found him a limited and weak Commander: 'The higher art of war is beyond him. I'm under no delusions whatsoever as to his ability to conduct large-scale operations in the field. He knows nothing about it. He's not a strong Commander and is incapable of giving firm and clear decisions as to what he wants. In fact no one ever knows what he *does* want, least of all his staff. He doesn't know himself. The whole truth of the matter is that Alexander has got a definitely limited brain, and doesn't understand the business.'

A less straightforward observer would not have been as honest about his 'very great friend' and Commanding Officer.

I remembered that in Sicily General Patton's Seventh Army was fighting alongside our Eighth as we landed, but during the campaign the Generals never met – which might explain why each ran his own private war. This Alexander accepted. The Eighth was struggling up the east coast against newly-arrived German divisions while Patton's army ushered the Germans into a happy escape around Etna. Both Commanders were prima donnas – though after that it was hard to detect any similarity in thought or action.

In the Mediterranean and later in France, even the affable

Supreme Commander General Eisenhower – who had never commanded men in battle – usually found Monty's infallibility hard to take.

As shipmates running the E-boat gauntlet for eight hours, Monty and I got along happily. This I believe was mainly because I told him what he wanted to hear. My thoughtful contribution was usually 'Yes, Sir.' That always went down well.

Although he was not chatty, and too correct to go into details, it was apparent Monty, like Alexander, was not much impressed by his new allies. The confusion on the Salerno beaches, the near-shambles when plans began to go wrong, the lack of aggressive spirit shown by Headquarters staff . . . few recent experiences had escaped the cold eye of the British perfectionist.

After sandwich, bun and apple, he went aft to stare at the waves whipping by – and doubtless to plan future battles; I went for'ard to watch out for the black silhouettes of hungry E-boats intent upon the war's biggest prize.

We arrived at the quiet beach we had left twelve hours earlier; the whole hazardous operation had been completed by the RN without a shot or a torpedo being fired, and Monty + 1 were both safe. After that adventure, our careers diverged. He went on to liberate western Europe, to be created a Viscount and a Field Marshal with a chestful of honours. I went on to capture the HQ of the German SS and get Mentioned in Despatches; small beer – but at least we both lived through it all . . .

Stimulated by the concern of Generals, the advance guard of the Eighth Army fought its way some 200 miles north in 13 days to relieve the hard-pressed Fifth, allowing them to push-on towards Naples – which General Clark was anxious to be seen liberating. Against weakening German resistance, commandos and paratroops stormed the mountains to the northwest of Vietri which commanded the defile through to Naples. The enemy withdrew, the beaches were saved, the bridgehead secure – so far.

The fact that some of our best Generals were being taken away from the theatre and returned to England in preparation for *Overlord*, the invasion of Normandy, may have had something to do with our apparent lack of direction. Generals Eisenhower, Montgomery, Bradley and Air Chief Marshal Tedder left for London, along with several veteran British and American formations.

Remaining in Italy, General Alexander then had seven Eighth Army divisions and thirteen Fifth Army divisions: five American, five British, two French and one Polish. Kesselring had 18 divisions.

The Italian surrender brought total confusion to Government offices from Rome to Brindisi – the temporary capital. Calls to the Italian War Office from military headquarters all over the country asked whether they should fight the Germans or not? They were answered by junior staff: 'Sorry – there's no one here.'

Very soon there *was* someone there: the German army. Within a week it had disarmed 56 Italian divisions, partially disarmed 29 others, and captured those 600,000 soldiers.

A supporting army fighting behind the lines would have made an enormous difference to the balance of the war but the Italians, never anxious for battle, received no orders or encouragement from us.

Their Navy, always professional, swiftly sailed away from Italy to escape the Germans, as agreed in the armistice terms. Four battleships and six cruisers surrendered in Malta and were greeted with full military honours by the Royal Navy. The Luftwaffe expressed its fury by bombing and sinking the Admiral's flagship, the cruiser *Roma,* with the loss of 1400 men.

On July 19 the US Air Force had hit the Rome railway mar-
shalling yards. The decision to drop 1,000 bombs on the outskirts
of the Eternal City was taken by the combined Chiefs of Staff
because the two vast yards were the hub of all rail movement
between north and south Italy. This Allied attack spread considerable public panic. The USAAF bombed Rome again on
August 13, and next day the Italian Government declared Rome
an Open City. Three weeks later Italy surrendered, and two days
after that the German Army occupied Rome – Open or Closed.

King Emmanuel's Government was transferred to Salerno. In
Feb '44 the Allies returned authority for the whole of southern
Italy to the Italian administration. There were then three Italys:
Southern Italy, occupied by the Allies; Central Italy, which
remained under German rule until the summer of '44; and
Northern Italy which until April '45 was the theatre of the
struggle by Allies and partisans against the Fascists of the Salò
Republic, and the Germans.

The role of Italians in this confused struggle for liberation
is usually dismissed. In fact from September 9 until the end of
the war, 72,500 military and civilians were killed and 40,000
wounded. There were believed to be some 360,000 partisans and
patriots fighting with little direction, but most of them on our
side.

Definitely on our side, thank goodness, were the Goumiers – a
little-known group with considerable impact. Our armies were
well-equipped in almost every way, with one surprising omission:
apart from the Gurkhas of the Indian divisions, we had no troops
trained in mountain warfare – unlike the Germans, who had an
LI Mountain Corps.

An odd exclusion this, as we were fighting our way up a chain
of 800 miles of Apennines, from the Straits of Messina to the
Alps, by way of everywhere. This great mass of mountains

bisecting the centre of Italy always seemed to cut through the heart of our battle lines of fighting soldiers – some of whom had probably never seen a mountain until they faced a towering range soaring up to 9,000 feet. Putting townsfolk to fight through such majestic scenery must have slowed our advance – certainly it made supplying troops dug into the skyline a task sometimes even beyond mules.

General Alphonse Juin, commanding the Corps Expédition-naire Français in the international Fifth Army, trumped everyone by introducing the Goumiers – 12,000 formidable fighters recruited from the Berber tribes of North Africa's Atlas moun-tains, with French officers and NCOs. He launched them across the trackless peaks and savage hills west from Ausonia. Preferring mules to jeeps, knives to rifles, and used to far more serious mountains, they saw the Apennines as foothills through which they moved as to the manner born.

I remember standing in front of vast wall maps at VI Corps headquarters in the catacombs of Nettuno, checking to see if there was any movement on the Front around Cassino. On a long horizontal map of Italy's boot, sideways, there was a vertical line across Italy showing exactly how far the Fifth and Eighth had got in their struggle to advance. The Intelligence officer briefing me then turned and walked a few paces to one lone dot on the map miles ahead of the static front line. 'That's the Goums' he said.

They were fighting alone, having left every other unit standing. These skilled and fearless tribesmen had one considerable disad-vantage to outsiders – sometimes even to their own officers: an instinctive and barely controlled savagery. Goums would descend upon a friendly or an enemy village and rape everyone in sight:

women, men, children, animals. . . Often they formed queues.

All this was standard – but not as we knew it. Italian peasants in villages through which they fought said they suffered far more in 24 hours of Goumier occupation than during eight months under the Germans.

They were a military success – though not if you were living in their path. Neighbouring units much preferred the old-style steady plod through the mountains; they admired the Goums' natural skills, but few were at ease with them. Even on our side, they were not easy to like.

A PASSING GLANCE AT PARADISE . . .

Capri lies three miles from the Italian mainland with a magnificent view of the Bay of Salerno and so a ringside seat at the war's toughest and most dramatic assault landing. This dominant position was pointless because the island was just not interested in conflict. Apart from a couple of dormant anti-aircraft batteries and a German radio station, it ignored any fighting anywhere, following a tradition of escapism established at the time of the Roman Empire.

For a passing glance at paradise, we landed by ferry at the Marina. A scramble of tourist-touts descended offering the regulation peacetime excursions around their miniscule haven, two-miles-by-four. The Blue Grotto? Up to Anacapri? The villa where Emperor Tiberius enjoyed various antisocial vices? The more innocent home of Gracie Fields?

Inland, the tiny Piazzetta remained brilliant and ridiculously theatrical, its little tables filling at noon with the surviving international smart-set, wartime edition, lured by the seductions of the island. Among such elegance were far more gaily-dressed women than men – who were younger and even smoother, with smaller wristwatches. It was the Roman Emperor Augustus who had first noticed the 'sweet idleness' of Capri, and it would take more than a world war to affect that balmy attitude among this blend of races untroubled by national ties.

The café chatter was full of happy laughter, though one subject was never approached: the War. I sensed it would be bad form to bring it up. There was a mild preoccupation with the shortage of bread which had to be brought across from the mainland, but at least there was plenty of cake, beautifully presented. Marie Antoinette would have appreciated the situation perfectly.

With some Correspondent friends I dined at the lovely home of a French resident. We had heard that an announcement of vital importance was to be broadcast from Radio Rome that evening, and were concerned. We were playing truant for a couple of days in paradise when we should have been at war, so were displeased that our cover was about to be blown. The prospect of some big story breaking while our backs were turned made us feel even more guilty. We waited anxiously.

Finally after much martial music the radio announced: 'The Government of Marshal Badoglio . . . has declared war on Germany!'

'My God' cried our hostess, exasperated, 'Is that *all?*' She switched back to dance music. That was Capri in October '43.

Later that night we again passed through the Piazzetta on our way back to reality. It was crammed with socialising Caprese, still refusing to pay any attention to the war, however close. They had chosen not to notice that a few miles north even their sort of civilisation was being saved by men in landing craft fighting and dying across the muddy Volturno River under a chill grey October sky.

* * *

As we all know, the Italians are a delightful race: good company, extremely stylish and rightly proud of their ancestors and their gorgeous country; but not even their greatest admirers would say that they were successful soldiers, these days. Even Mussolini noticed. After their surrender in Libya his son-in-law and Foreign Minister, Count Ciano, told him, 'With an Army like *ours* we can only declare war on Peru.' Unaccustomed to the truth, Mussolini stored that away.

In Rome, King Emmanuel had called a meeting of the Grand Council in July '43 to remove Mussolini and replace him with Marshal Badoglio. Count Ciano was one of those who supported this dismissal. Six months later, after his rescue from hotel-arrest at Gran Sasso, a resurrected Mussolini did not choose to spare his favourite daughter's husband when he was tried by a Tribunal in Verona and sentenced to death for 'attempting to destroy the independence of the State . . . and giving aid and comfort . . . to the enemy.' Ciano was executed by firing squad at Fort Procolo, outside Verona. He died bravely.

After waiting until June 10 1940 to declare war on the Allies in a belated scramble for spoils, Mussolini, the man who (as we always said) made the trains run on time and drained the Pontine Marshes, the Duce's speeches brandished Italy's eight million bayonets. This was the usual bellicose nonsense from the balcony of Rome's Palazzo Venezia.

In fact the Italian Army boasted about 79 divisions, though only nineteen were complete with men and arms, and most of the rifles were made in 1891 – even older than ours. Much of their equipment was imaginary, though they *did* have 1900 antiquated aircraft, and 400 3½-ton tanks. The German Tiger tank, at 57 tons, weighed more than 40 Rolls-Royces; the Italian pocket tank, a few Minis. No wonder Hitler was unimpressed. It was bad enough on our side of the scales: Shermans only weighed 35 tons.

Facing us when we landed in Sicily had been a massive Italian army – somewhere. In truth we hardly noticed it, for all its ranks were deeply nervous, had no idea *why* they were fighting and just wanted to go home and forget the whole uncomfortable business.

Naples had fallen on October 1 amid a clamour of urchins shouting at our armoured cars for food and hungry women offering themselves for a packet of biscuits. Following our bombings and German demolition, it seemed a dead city of shuttered shops. Even the high-pressure Neapolitan salesmen were out of action. The wide harbour was clogged by the wrecks of 130 ships, and the retreating Germans had blown-up and booby-trapped the city's sewage and water systems. Typhus arrived instantly.

Naples has always had a tenuous and insecure grasp upon health and hygiene. Thirty years later, a cholera outbreak in 1973 was to reveal that the city had no sewers, yet was living contentedly around its beautiful but poisoned bay. The popular saying, 'See Naples and die' was meant to summon visitors to enjoy its ramshackle charms, but took on a forbidding significance with every passing plague.

General Mark Clark was displeased because he had planned a grand entry into the city when he would acknowledge the plaudits of welcoming crowds – a sort of curtain-raiser for Rome. He wrote in his Memoirs that there was little triumph in his journey through the deserted streets of 'a city of ghosts'. He gave a Liberation celebration, but nobody showed.

The always surprising stoicism of the Neapolitans soon surfaced and the shops began to open for business, though with little on display. Neapolitan shopkeepers were of course cannier than those in other towns who, before remembering to put up their prices, sold their remaining stocks to eager Allied soldiers enjoying the benevolent rate of exchange. In Naples they waited weeks or months before emptying the storeroom and adding zeros to the price tags.

A few good harbourside restaurants around the famous *Zit Theresa* opened, with costly menus. They offered a good four-course meal with wine for 140 lire, or seven shillings. Only the military – or black marketeers – could afford such outrageous prices.

One private enterprise flourished as never before. Naples had long been known as the capital of major and minor thievery, a lifestyle stimulated by war. Now beneficent Allied merchant ships arrived daily with food and army supplies, their crews not geared to deal with mass and well-organised criminality which in a hungry lawless land had become woven into every life. It was calculated that one third of all supplies landed at this major port was instantly stolen, to reappear in the black market. So it was Christmas every day for the gangsters of the Camorra.

The emerging shopkeepers of the Via Roma were followed by the friendly Neapolitan signorinas. So effusive was their more private welcome that notices soon went up along roads into the city: 'Dangerous type of VD in this area.' We never discovered where the safe type was.

Public Relations settled happily into the Villa Ruffo on Posillipo Hill, a stately mansion overlooking the bay, with Vesuvius – the terror and the pride of the city – smoking peacefully in the distance. This was a spectacular setting of style and comfort amid the tarnished splendour of Naples, though our billet became unkindly known as Villa Rough-it. I would happily have roughed-it indefinitely, but needed to return to the Eighth

Army, still trying to push north up the east coast of Italy, 140 miles away.

An unopposed landing by the 1st Airborne Division at Taranto had been followed by the liberation of Brindisi and then the major port on the ankle of Italy, Bari, a Fascist stronghold.

The ironies of life at a warfront when you're living on a razor's-edge between stiff-upper-lip badinage, and death – the injustice, the unfairness of it all – was underlined for me in this Adriatic port. We arrived in Bari just after the Italian surrender and found it untouched and, like Capri, quite indifferent to war.

We were particularly irritated by the many Italian Army officers in ornate uniforms strutting about the boulevards wearing their revolvers, and lounging in pavement cafés like the cast of a Drury Lane musical. We – the victors – had been fighting the Germans, sleeping in ditches and unable to bathe; now it was infuriating to find ourselves patronised and dismissed by defeated posturing pseudo-soldiers in this unscathed city, who had never heard a gun fire. What's more, they also had to live-down a worse record than the Germans in their treatment of prisoners.

Much boorishness survived. The posh Hotel Imperiale refused to give a room to the Allied Tactical Air Commander in Italy, Air Vice Marshal Sir Arthur Coningham. This was unwise. The irate New Zealander promptly commandeered an entire floor for the RAF.

On the plus side, the shops in their city were still stuffed with goods that at our victor's exchange-rate seemed encouragingly cheap: a pair of rare silk stockings and a bottle of Asti Spumante to go with them, 4s.6d each. Chanel No 5 as a going-away present – 15s. The rate at the top local brothel was seven lire – then less than tuppence and, I was told, usually worth every penny. None of these bargains survived the frantic inflation which arrived soon after as Italians chased the rate of exchange, and won.

Disregarding, in the main, such inexpensive distractions, the Eighth pushed forward up the east coast of Italy, attempting to relieve the pressure on the desperate Fifth.

A popular silver-haired public relations officer, Captain Sir Gerald Boles, reminded us how our warfront lives were ruled by luck. We would sometimes find ourselves working alongside our brother War Correspondents – civilians in uniform who were taken around in the Humber Pullmans of Public Relations by Conducting Officers. They were usually subalterns recovering from wounds or officers regarded as dispensable by their units. One was Sir Gerald and he, to put a fine point upon it, was allergic to lead. He was deeply anxious not to be killed – injured, even. In a charming and patrician manner he would shy away from the most distant explosion.

While escorting Correspondents around the Front in search of their stories, he refused to go anywhere near the fighting. 'Might get the Humber damaged,' he would explain, apologetically. 'War Department property, you know.'

It was true that PR only had a few Pullmans left from the desert, and that some Correspondents were quite content to go along with his careful timidity and fight-the-good-fight only upon their portable typewriters; but the more gung-ho reporters would not be fobbed off by the gentility of 'Sir Gerald and Lady Boles', as Ted Gilling called him scornfully. They were missing all the action and the subsequent stories. After indignant protests from the Press it was decided that Sir Gerald had to go.

He was too endearing a man to humiliate by RTUing, by returning to his unit, so his seniors cast around for an acceptably safe job away from the Front where Sir Gerald could pursue a gentler life undisturbed by explosives. They finally decided to send him back to Bari. This port was then miles behind the Front, but a sufficient number of Correspondents were passing through on their way to Yugoslavia and the Balkans to justify the posting.

With touching relief he turned his back on the war, leaving his brother officers to get on with what could be quite a dangerous role – without, as it transpired, further casualties. Sir Gerald drove south and settled into a sea view suite in a comfortable harbourside hotel to sit-out the rest of the war peacefully in that tranquil unscathed city.

In a surprise Luftwaffe raid a few nights after his arrival, an ammunition ship anchored in the harbour outside his hotel suffered a direct hit. It exploded and sank, taking sixteen other ships with it. The blast was felt for 20 miles. Sir Gerald was blown through several walls, and into eternity.

I always enjoyed the 'Sign Wars' which could relieve the monotony of any journey. There were the useful warnings: 'Dust Brings Shells', the rather laboured, 'If you go any further, take a Cross with you.' Even the decisive, 'Don't be a bloody fool.' Should you pass one saying *'Achtung! Strasse liegt unter Feuer!'* it meant, roughly translated, 'You've come too far – turn round and get the Hell out of here.'

In another category there were those which gave units a chance to publicise their achievements, or get their own back. All Americans were keen on public relations – drivers were always being 'Welcomed' to some village or river crossing 'by courtesy of' a US Infantry regiment which was just doing its job. Often it seemed we were on Route 66 and would soon be offered a giant hamburger.

On one mountain road where as usual the Germans had blown every bridge, the first replacement had a large sign saying proudly, 'You are Crossing this Bridge by Courtesy of the US Fifth Army Engineers who Built it in 3 Days 14 Hours and 26 Minutes!'

At the next blown river-crossing the familiar British Bailey bridge had a small notice: 'This Bridge was built by the REs in 9 Hours 42 Minutes'. Underneath in brackets and small print: ('There is *nothing* unusual about this bridge'). They must have been the Sappers who invented Cool.

There was also the tantalising problem of naming defensive Lines – and the enemy had plenty. To infantrymen the war in Italy was one fortified German Line after another. Break through one and there was always the next, just ahead. Ford a river – and there's its twin, behind an identical mountain. We had the Attila Line, the Caesar Line, the Bernhard Line, the Trasimene Line, the Barbara Line, the Olga and Lydia Lines, the Paola and Mädchen Lines ... As the battle moved north it seemed the Germans were thinking more of home and the wife, even amid the big-time Gothic and Gustav Lines built for the Todt organisation by Italian prisoners.

A name had to be resonant, defiant, gallant and worth fighting for. So to restore the billing it was obvious that a major line *should* have been named after the Führer – heads were due to roll. The Adolf Hitler Line needed to be the most brave and steadfast of them all. This would please everyone back at Command in Berlin.

So fortunately when the formidable Gustav Line was breached, the Germans had just established a deeper defence running across the Liri Valley, near Pontecorvo and Aquino – at last, the Hitler Line!

This blocked any Allied movement along Highway 6 and up the valley. It was even more substantial than the Gustav and featured permanent concrete works, the turrets of Panther tanks buried in the ground at key points, and 75mm guns. Every defensive position was, as usual, cleverly sited.

Then suddenly in January '44 the significant Adolf Hitler Line was renamed the Senger Line, after the Commander of the 14th Panzer Corps responsible for the defence of Monte Cassino, Lieutenant General Fridolin von Senger und Etterlin.

The reason for that urgent name change was not too subtle. Someone had read the runes – and the future was uncertain. A defensive line liable to be humiliatingly breached by Allied armies – or even worse, ignored (remember the Maginot Line?) could not be allowed to go down under the name of the Führer. Generals had been executed for less. Fridolin would doubtless be more amenable, so he was in the charts for a few weeks. He must have been thoughtful and accommodating for he tried to save the Abbey of Monte Cassino, was a Rhodes scholar at Oxford and reportedly disliked Hitler.

That name change was fortunate for some, and just in time. The Senger Line crumbled – indeed General Clark became concerned lest its quick penetration by the Eighth might lead to a sudden dash to Rome. He would much rather see his own Fifth Army held down and savaged than have the Eighth triumphant on his Road to Rome . . .

I missed much of the fun and games of Naples and Bari because in that bleak winter the Army was being decimated, not by Germans but by jaundice.

This spread through all ranks and did far more damage than high explosives. First it made you feel like death, while you still looked fine. Then you turned bright yellow and felt fine, while looking like death. It was a confusing and unpleasant plague.

I was carried by ambulance many uncomfortable miles from the snow-covered mountains of central Italy, south to Bari – to experience the first flight of my life. It was not stylish. I was in the middle of a stack of stretchers in a packed Red Cross DC3 which flew back to Catania in Sicily, then on to Tunis. After this an ambulance train took me across the border to Constantine in Algeria and finally, a truck on to hospital to start treatment. By then I was almost well again.

Strange that the first of the many millions of airborne miles I was to cover around *Whicker's World* during my lifetime should have been endured lying flat on my back. Now of course you pay *extra* to travel like that.

STRUGGLING TO GET TICKETS FOR THE FIRST CASUALTY LIST . . .

The Anzio Experience has remained with me, mainly because I never expected to live through it. One retains a proprietorial attitude towards any hazardous expedition experienced totally, from planning to victory. Having invaded Sicily and then the mainland of Italy, I'd had two lucky invasions and was hoping the next assault landing would complete my quota: Third Time *still* Lucky.

I had worked my way back to the Front line from the hospital in Algeria, three or four countries away, and rejoined AFPU on the east coast of Italy just in time for the unit Christmas party. This was as jolly as could be, considering our billet: the Vasto Theological College.

On that Adriatic sector I joined one of the best divisions in the Eighth Army, the 78th 'Battleaxe' Division which had fought its way here from Medjez-el-Bab in Tunisia and was now being replaced in the line by an old partner, the tough 1st Canadian Division. To capture the gaunt mountain town of Ortona they faced the entrenched 1st Parachute Division, most disciplined and feared of Kesselring's armies. It was the battle of champions.

The Canadians took over the Front on the evening of

December 20 to fight amid the freezing ruins. In bitter struggles lone houses were captured and surrendered and recaptured. Only the piles of dead were changed. They were still fighting there on Christmas Day. The Paras brought up flame-throwers with a 60-yard range which they used in attack and defence through the ruined town.

The Canadian answer was to call in Sherman tanks as close-support wherever the narrow streets allowed, and six-pounder anti-tank guns that shot through or demolished ancient stone walls.

In this grotesque Christmas battle with its stark backdrop, it took the Canadians eight desperate days to capture Ortona. By then both sides were exhausted. The last Paras were finally cleared out on December 28, though for days afterwards Canadians were killed or maimed by the mines and booby-traps they had buried in the ruined homes of that desolate mountain town.

The capture brought that offensive to an end. The Army was tired, weakened by losses and could see no military objective ahead except – on the other coast – the major prize of Rome, but that was in the path of the Fifth Army. On the Adriatic we had fought ourselves to a winter stalemate.

Then an urgent message from AFHQ sent me jeeping through the mountains to Naples yet again – following the action. There I learned I was to command cameramen covering the landing of 50,000 British and American troops behind enemy lines, south of Rome. The intention was to cut Highway 6 and the railway supply-lines to the Monte Cassino front where German para-troops were still resisting strongly, to trap Kesselring's Tenth and Fourteenth Armies, and finally to liberate Rome.

With Geoffrey Keating I drove out to Castellammare, the port across the bay from Naples where most of the armada was assembling, to place sergeant-cameramen with units in the first wave of our assault. We had to negotiate with the senior officer commanding the loading of the invasion fleet, because as usual there was not space for everyone who needed to go, and although we saw our role as important it was hard to compete against fighting units, gunners or ambulances.

To jolly the Colonel along, Keating suggested that I take a few personal pictures of him in action – gentle harmless flattery. Pleased with such attention he became more amenable, and subsequently agreed to most of our requests for space and accommodation.

It was curious to be so eager to join an expedition that offered applicants the probability of injury or death as the reward for success. It felt like struggling to get tickets for a First Night, when the winners would probably end up in the first casualty list of permanent Losers.

Afterwards Geoffrey said he would get my pictures developed. I explained that, as usual, I had no film in the camera. We could not take pictures of everyone we met, and it was doubtful whether we would ever see the Colonel again. This was a bit naughty, but practical; we could not burden our hard-pressed Developing Section with social shots not for publication. 'Red-hots,' we called them, and they never amused our shy colleague Len Puttnam – father of Lord Puttnam-to-be – who ran the developers and coped manfully with our output.

Geoffrey, more experienced than I, said 'Fatal mistake. Now you're going to run into that Colonel everywhere, for the rest of the war. You'll always be making excuses.' He was right – so I never did *that* again.

On January 21 '44 an armada of 374 ships sailed out to sea, then turned to starboard and steamed north. This was Operation *Shingle*. We had a fair idea where we might be going because Neapolitan spivs on the Via Roma and around the docks had been selling postcards of Anzio, a place of which I had then never heard.

The weather was perfect, the sea smooth – but we knew German radio had been discussing an Allied landing behind their lines. We prepared for another Salerno bloodbath.

At nightfall troops on our ship wrapped themselves in blankets and tried to sleep on deck. In the wardroom, officers played poker for ridiculously high stakes, trying to get rid of cash. Just when there was no need for money I could not stop winning, of course – so landed with pockets bulging with lire which took months to spend. It was the first (and last) time I have faced that problem.

Our vast armada came to anchor off the small resort and port of Anzio – just as the Neapolitans had forecast. As we dropped anchor in a crisp dawn, braced for enemy reaction, I went below decks for my guide book, to learn that Anzio had been a flourishing commercial city in 490 BC and was the birthplace of the Emperor Nero and the home of Caligula. I *do* like to know where I'm invading.

Viewed from the deck of our LST at dawn it seemed a pleasant little fishing port bordered by low-rise blocks and villas along the coast, and some substantial patrician homes amid the pines and sand dunes. It had already been damaged by our supporting fire – and much worse was to come.

Along the coast, neighbouring Nettuno looked older, with wine caves at its heart – soon to be taken over by VI Corps as a secure HQ, with life-saving cellars attached. Caligula had wanted to turn Anzio into the capital of the Roman Empire, and Popes and nobles followed his enthusiasms. The fall of the Roman Empire led to Anzio's decline for centuries, until the 1700s when

Cardinal Antonio Pignatelli, returning by sea from Naples to Rome, sheltered from a storm in Nero's old port and believed his life had been spared. He promised if he became Pope he would rebuild the place – and was a man of his word.

So Anzio had its ups and downs. Unfortunately, I arrived in time for a major Down. After our landing the port area was shelled and bombed by the Germans, night and day for four months. At least it became famous, once again.

To get here during the night our massive fleet had sailed past the Gustav Line and in the distance, Monte Cassino, which now lay 80 miles behind us. The harbour was suddenly busy with warships. Barrage balloons tethered to the larger craft floated protectively above our armada. Destroyers cut through the fleet, laying thick black smokescreens. Further out to sea big cruisers moved ponderously around in semi-circles, rocking as their thunderous broadsides supported our landing.

Red air raid warning flags flew almost permanently – yet we had some 2,000 aircraft in the theatre, the Luftwaffe only 350. Sometimes the RAF or the USAAF held off the attackers, but usually they got through to drop their bombs and hurtle away, low over the water.

The two Navies staged a useful diversion by bombarding Rome's seaport, Civitavecchia, 75 miles further north. There they carried-out a fake landing so impressive that Kesselring ordered that all harbour facilities should be demolished immediately.

I went in with the 1st 'White Triangle' Division on to Peter Beach, just north of Anzio, a broad sandy expanse between sea and dunes stretching towards Ostia and the enticing target of Rome, a mere 33 miles away. The platoon I was landing with that sunny morning was confident and cheerful. The light return-fire had been spasmodic. They were all businesslike and, like me, beginning to feel they had done it all before and knew their way around a landing beach.

What they did not know, of course, was that during the next months at Anzio their division would lose 100 officers and more than 1,000 other ranks. Another 400 officers and 8,000 men would be casualties, or missing.

After our cheerful landing the division would lose 60 per cent of its officers, 50 per cent of its men, but as the warm water and soft clean sand of Peter Beach splashed up to meet our feet such a terrible future was, fortunately, unthinkable.

The US 3rd Division was landing on X-Ray Beach, south of Nettuno, where resistance was also light: the usual 88mm shells and air raids. Most of our early casualties were from wooden box mines hidden in the sand, which fooled the Royal Engineers' metal-detectors.

I never lost my horror of mines, nor my admiration for the courage of the REs who went ahead and defused them by the thousand. The thought of sudden death springing up from the sand to grab and remove my vitals was an ever-present night-mare, as was the memory of regimental aid posts trying to cope with men without feet or legs who minutes before had been slogging cheerfully up the beach.

General Eisenhower recalled once telling the Russian Army Commander, Marshal Zhukov, of the intricate and extravagant devices introduced by the allied armies to clear minefields – like those great flails on the front of some British tanks. The jolly little ruler of the Red armies – perhaps the greatest Field Commander of World War II – found all those elaborate precautions time-wasting and unnecessary. The quickest and most effective way of clearing a minefield, the Marshal explained, was to assemble a battalion of infantry and order them to march straight across it.

That cruel order was not a comfortable recollection as we

prepared to cover a hundred yards of smooth sand, and then the more threatening dunes. In any AFPU pictures of our troops landing on Peter Beach, I'm the one on tiptoe . . .

The first Germans we met on landing were the 200 who had been sent to Anzio to rest and recover from the fighting at Cassino. Most of them were asleep when they got a wake-up call from a different enemy. Once again we had achieved surprise. The Germans had expected an attack further north, where our feint went in. They were wrong again.

So were we. After a perfect landing in enemy territory, almost nothing went *right*. The roads to Rome and the commanding hills were open – but we did not choose to take them.

By the evening Major General John P. Lucas, Commander of VI Corps, had landed 36,000 of us, with 3,200 vehicles. He did not land himself until the next day, when he moved into his command cellar in Nettuno; and there he stayed.

I learned afterwards from Prince Stefano Borghese, whose Palace overlooked Anzio harbour, that the ominous approaching rumble of hundreds of ships' engines out at sea had been heard long before our devastating support barrage began, but the German Harbourmaster thought it was his supply ships returning from Livorno.

After an hour ashore that invasion day my first courier left to carry back to Naples the exposed film we had shot. Our first mishap came when a bomb blew Sergeant Lambert off the quayside. He landed in the water still clutching his bag of film, but no serious harm was done. Just as in a battle zone when any aircraft landing you can walk away from is a good landing, so any naval episode you can *swim* away from is quite acceptable, in the circumstances.

We headed our preparatory dope sheets: 'The Liberation of Rome'. Our cautious target was, Rome in ten days. I told my cameramen to hoard film stock for the excitement of bringing freedom to the first Axis capital. As soon as I could get my jeep ashore I started up the Via Anziate heading for Rome, with any luck, and those first triumphant pictures. We were some 60 miles *ahead* of the German army, which for some reason after all our backs-to-the-wall battles seemed rather hilarious. I resisted the euphoric desire to drive fast through the open countryside, singing.

The flat farmland seemed deserted, yet I could hear sounds of battle ... After some miles I was beginning to suspect the Seven Hills of Rome must be just around the corner. Then at a road junction before the River Moletta some Sherman tanks were hull-down behind a fly-over, firing over it. The supporting 1st Battalion of the Loyals had been held up by enemy fire. Snipers' bullets hissed past as we watched the shelling they had called down on to enemy-held houses.

That was to be the limit of our advance upon Rome. I did not foresee we had walked into a death trap and would be fighting for our lives for eighteen desperate weeks.

The Germans' reaction had been swift and almost overwhelming. As usual, they were surprised but not panicked, though Hitler – always keen on other people fighting to the death – was taking our assault landing personally. He appreciated the propaganda impact of such an invasion and his reaction would resonate from the *Oberkommando der Wehrmacht* in Berlin to the beaches of Anzio.

Reserve divisions were rushed-in from around Italy and Yugo-slavia, paratroops flown in from France. By midnight Kesselring had assembled 20,000 men around Anzio, with many more on the way. Artillery positions had been established 3,000 feet up in the Alban Hills, dominating beaches and port. This was not going to be another walkover for us – indeed it became one of the most desperate and costly campaigns of World War II, and a near-disaster.

Hitler, braced for the fall of Rome and cataclysmic battles in Russia, knew that for the Allies a bridgehead defeat would be a frightening reminder that the Wehrmacht could still prove invincible. It would show the world that an Allied Second Front could be thrown back into the English Channel. It could force the delay or even the cancellation of D-Day.

He repeated in his Order of the Day that there must be no surrender: 'Fight with bitter hatred an enemy who conducts a ruthless war of annihilation against the German people . . .' He was evidently determined that the Wehrmacht should defend Rome with the fatal obstinacy displayed at Stalingrad. 'The Führer expects the bitterest struggle for every yard.' This would threaten the destruction of the Eternal City.

If Hitler was displeased with the battle so far, it was as nothing compared to the carefully suppressed anger of Churchill when the initial success of the combined operation he had encouraged was frittered-away by inexperienced or timid Generals. The isolated Anzio pocket of the US VI Corps was not racing to relieve the Fifth Army at Cassino, as planned, or driving triumphantly up Rome's Via Veneto, but was itself trapped, besieged and liable to be pushed back into the sea.

It was an ill-planned operation which Churchill had rescued from the official graveyard of discarded military adventures. He had secretly believed the bridgehead might exorcise the ghosts of another disastrous landing: Suvla Bay in Gallipoli, 1915, which cost him his portfolio at the Admiralty. He afterwards admitted, 'Anzio was my worst moment of the war – and I had most to do with it. I did not want two Suvla Bays in one lifetime.'

That evening we were still held up at the flyover, so I went back to Peter Beach to look for my sergeants. As I arrived, another hit-and-run fighter-bomber came in. Suddenly out at sea the air shuddered and against the darkening sky a sheet of orange flame spread across the horizon. A bomb had hit the destroyer *Janus*, which exploded and sank in 20 minutes with the loss of 150 men. The flame died quickly, leaving only an angry glare against the night sky.

As one of the attacking aircraft roared away over our heads, Bofors shells hit its tail. Every man on the beach was cheering as it crashed and exploded – but it was poor exchange for a destroyer and so many lives.

We did not know it at the time, but the drive for Rome, the Alban Hills and Cassino had not even been contemplated by our Commander, a grizzled and amiable American known as Corncob Charlie. A bespectacled artilleryman who enjoyed the poetry of Rudyard Kipling, Major General John Lucas was 54 but seemed as old and benevolent as Father Christmas – though less active.

The Germans knew far more than we did about what was happening, because in a major stroke of luck one of their Allied prisoners was found to be carrying a copy of the entire *Shingle* Plan. This instantly confirmed Kesselring's conviction that Lucas would not even attempt to cut his supply lines with Cassino.

He had ordered every unit to dig-in and consolidate – when they could have driven unopposed into the surrounding hills and cut Kesselring's communications to the south. General Mark Clark cancelled the use of the US 504th Parachute Regiment along with the jump by an airborne division on to Rome Airport. The whole operation became stagnant, with commando raids discouraged and all effort concentrated upon defence. Fifty thousand troops were not enough for an attack, it seemed; we had to dig-in and await reinforcements. The Germans, meanwhile, had eighteen divisions south of Rome and were anxious to use them.

Lucas did not think of Rome, he thought of Gallipoli, Tobruk and Dunkirk, of desperate defeat. In the first 48 hours our initial Anzio victory was thrown-away. This is where we needed the fire-eating fast-moving General Patton.

During the planning for *Shingle,* General Lucas had confessed to his diary his nervousness about the Anzio operation, 'This whole affair has a strong odour of Gallipoli, and apparently the same amateur (Churchill) is still on the coach's bench.' When he risked voicing that opinion to the Allied Naval Commander-in-Chief Mediterranean, Admiral Sir John Cunningham, he got a sharp sailor's reaction: 'If that's how you feel you'd better resign.' He did not.

Even Lucas's Commander, General Mark Clark, had warned him 'not to stick his neck out' the way *he* had (he said) at Salerno. He was telling Lucas to fight the battle as he saw fit, but it is incredible that such a cautious and unenterprising General should have been chosen to lead a daring operation demanding dash and drive. However, this advice may have been influenced by Clark's determination to liberate Rome himself. He did not want some bemused subordinate arriving there first, after a lucky punch.

We had achieved surprise with our landing, so half the battle was won; but then the slow Allied exploitation and the intensity of the German reaction instantly recreated the equilibrium, and the attacking British and Americans fell back into the submissive posture of a besieged garrison.

The Germans were amazed we made no move; surely it was unthinkable that we should do *nothing?* With such cooperation they had little difficulty in containing us. Their reaction to our invasion became almost overwhelming: within days seven divisions had been rushed in to surround us, including Panzers with Tiger tanks.

British commanders were seething with frustration at their enforced inaction. Up in the front line I found Guardsmen brewing-up and their officers playing bridge, while awaiting orders. They should have been racing for Rome.

In Cairo, General Sir Henry Maitland Wilson ('Jumbo') who had just succeeded General Eisenhower as Allied Commander Mediterranean, made it clear to the Press – and to Kesselring – that he was going to defend, not attack. 'If the Germans run true to style, as they always do' he announced 48 hours after our landing, 'they will counter-attack our beachhead.' Thus he advertised our passive intentions to the enemy.

So all was not going well at Anzio. We had launched a major landing led by only two divisions, plus Commandos and US Rangers. At Salerno, with no surprise and no numerical dominance, we only just escaped being flung back into the sea, defeated. Clutching desperately at a landing beach an attacker initially needs total dominance, as General Montgomery well knew.

When Churchill first showed him the plan for *Overlord*, the Second Front in Normandy which he was to command when he left Italy, Montgomery's immediate reaction was, 'This will not do. I must have more in the initial punch.' D-Day in Normandy was to be in four months' time, and Churchill admitted, 'After considerable argument a whole set of arrangements was made in consequence of his opinion, which proved right.'

Montgomery's knowledge of the price we paid in Italy saved thousands of lives in Normandy. To escape such a stalemate the invasion planners could now demand greater strength for *Overlord*. They had learned the expensive lessons of Anzio.

From D + 1 even I could tell that if we were fortunate enough to hold on to our beachhead, we faced a long and desperate battle – so I requisitioned a large house overlooking the harbour.

It was a substantial three-storey lump of a place and – I noted approvingly – strongly built. It stood high over the seashore in front of the coast road. The front line was only seven miles away. At a push we could drive – or swim – out of trouble.

From its wide terrace we would get excellent pictures of our shipping being shelled and bombed – and doubtless, sunk. It was an ideal place for a billet and tripod position – but on the other hand it *was* at the heart of the German artillery's target area . . . I'd worry about that tomorrow.

From their observation posts in the Alban Hills enemy gunners could watch every inch of the beachhead, and look deep into our private lives. No man could move without being seen. Little wonder Corncob Charlie rarely left his HQ down in the caves of Nettuno.

In our barren seaside villa we too slept in the cellars until deciding that shells were preferable to rats, and moving back to the ground floor. Our rats were all fat and overconfident – and at a battlefront you knew exactly what they had been eating. Even upstairs I awoke one night to find an enormous rat staring at me across my feet. It was wondering what to do. I knew what to do. I reached for my bedside .38 and – hoping to miss my big toes – shot it.

That awoke the remainder of the unit who thought the Germans had landed. They were about to shoot-back through my door, just to be on the safe side . . .

Calm restored, Geoffrey Keating and I considered the drill, should the Germans ever come to call. We'd seen some tattered clothes in the garden shed and decided to wear these and head north for Rome, rather than attempt to get back to the Eighth Army through the German lines.

Major Keating, my CO, was a most unusual man. A devout Catholic and bon viveur, he had an extremely high threshold of pain, which could be disconcerting. He just did not seem to notice when violence or death was approaching. He had arrived in Egypt to run Montgomery's Army Film Unit and, indifferent to General Rommel and the Afrika Korps, began cheerfully swanning around the desert as though gate-crashing other Units' parties, blithely unconcerned about any battles going on around him. This of course meant he was never injured and survived to win an excellent Military Cross.

He never touched drink – though it might have sustained such a perilous lifestyle. One afternoon after the war Susie, a mutual friend, rang me at BBC Television Centre to say they had just got married ... This was another surprise. I had a table at Prunier's that evening so invited them along, if they had no plans.

Looking through the wine list for something interesting with which to toast his bride, Geoffrey settled for a cider, assuming it to be the softest of drinks and better with fish than a coke. After several country ciders he moved unsteadily towards the marriage bed, and from then on his life and social consumption changed direction. He never looked back – and his wife never forgave me.

At Anzio I went with him around our front-line positions and suddenly noticed that, while we were driving in his open jeep along an embankment, laughing and chatting, we were on the dreaded Lateral Road where nothing else moved. I remembered tanks rarely ventured along it in daylight because of heavy enemy artillery fire and German machine guns with sights locked-on to any movement.

We were looking for a Company HQ. There was no other traffic. Then I saw a few soldiers in the dugout positions below us. They were moving at a crouch or lying looking up at us as we drove happily along, an apparition in a no-go area. Just before the firing began, I realised we were not travelling sensibly.

Needless to say Geoffrey's reaction to possible death and destruction was so indifferent and outrageous that we emerged unscathed and drove on, still finding something or other funny; doubtless my growing panic.

I found out afterwards that Geoffrey would go to sleep in his dentist's chair during treatment. By then I had registered one firm Unit rule which saw me through the war: separate jeeps.

The bridgehead solidified along 16 miles of coast and about seven miles inland – say just over 100 square miles. I've known bigger farms. Some 20,000 Italian civilians had been shipped back to Naples, leaving Anzio a small and desperate military state and a throwback to the Great War days of static warfare, shelled all day and bombed all night. There was no hiding place at Anzio.

On most warfronts there is a calm secure area at the rear where the wounded can be taken, where units rest when they come out of the line and Generals may sleep comfortably. On the bridgehead there were no safe areas. You were never out of range.

Indeed soldiers at the front would sometimes refuse to report minor wounds which might mean they would be sent back to a field hospital – and so into the heavy artillery target area. Provided it was not a major battle they often felt more secure at the front, where the war was personal and the percentages could more easily be calculated.

Keating and I invited a number of friendly War Correspondents to escape from the barren Press camp next door and join us in our more substantial villa, which in our days of bombardment had already been recognised as Lucky. They included one of the Rabelaisian characters of our war, Reynolds Packard. In peaceful days he had been Rome Correspondent of the *Chicago Tribune,* and with his wife Eleanor had written a well-titled book on Mussolini, 'Balcony Empire'. He was knowledgeable, sociable and excellent company but had, we discovered, one foible liable to render him untouchable – even in our Mess.

The villa's sitting room, where we played poker and sometimes even worked, overlooked the sea and so faced away from arriving shells. It was always pleasantly crowded and noisy enough to discourage the rats, so this was where we set-up our camp beds each night. Reynolds, a portly funny figure, was a notable non-teetotaller and so able to sleep through most bombardments. His only lack of social grace was revealed when he woke in the night and needed to urinate. In the unfamiliar darkness he would struggle out of his bed – and pee wherever he stood.

He had been campaigning too long in open country, sleeping in too many fields without the benefit of indoor sanitation and his behaviour pattern had become lax, not to mention disgusting. Not too many people wanted the bed space next to him.

Such a reaction to a full bladder might be acceptable in a foxhole or on a beach, but was less welcome in our new Mess. After the deluge a chastened Packard would face fury in the morning. He could not deny the offence because the evidence was all too obvious. He was always horrified and full of remorse, blamed demon vino and swore it would never happen again. Next night, it would.

In the early hours we would awake to the sound of running water hitting the tiles. The first weary automatic move in the darkness was to lean down, rescue shoes, put them in the dry zone on the end of the bed, and go back to sleep. In the morning, an uproar of protest, another furious inquest and more craven apologies. The distasteful procedure was in danger of becoming normal.

Packard's momentary forgetfulness in the darkness of a strange room was not excusable – though perhaps understandable to those living on a war front where the niceties of civilised life could fall away. After some months campaigning in the field and living basically I committed a graceless mistake myself, which still haunts me.

We had been advancing slowly through Tuscany and sleeping rough; but once Florence fell some old friends invited me to a welcome party in their magnificent apartment on the Lungarno, overlooking the river. During that elegant evening in the sunlit drawing room I remember needing to stub out my cigarette. Seeing no ashtrays in the salon, I dropped it on to the deep-pile carpet and punctiliously ground it out with my toe – as one would.

As I turned to continue the conversation I had an uneasy feeling something was not *quite* right . . . but could not recollect what it might be.

It was not until later that night when my hostess upbraided me – 'I *saw* you' – that I was struck by the vast distance between surviving on a hillside, and living amid glowing Renaissance treasures. I had become one of the brutal and licentious. I paid in flowers, shame and guilt.

The free spirit of Reynolds Packard was even less socially acceptable, but eventually threats of expulsion began to wear him down, or dry him up. After a couple of weeks struggling with him *and* with the strengthening Wehrmacht now surrounding us, we were becoming familiar with the death-defying routines of life in an encircled battlefield – the deep daily depression that appeared each dawn. So Geoffrey and I decided it was time to attempt to be more social and civilised. Some warriors' relaxation would improve morale: we had mugs, a few glasses, we had whisky, gin and local vino; we even had American saltines and processed cheese. All told, our first party was indicated – the kind of promising social adventure that could make Anzio just endurable.

The one imperative for such a gathering was of course female – beyond price and almost impossible to discover in such a war zone. Almost, but not totally. The vast and impressive US 95th Evacuation Hospital had just established its dark green marquees with big red crosses, and the more secure stone squares covered with tarpaulins, along the coast-road to the south. It was decided that I should approach the Matron and offer her nurses the freedom of our Mess for one evening. Such an hospitable international gesture was the least we could do.

Making Matron see the good sense of this project was not easy, even at Anzio – *particularly* at Anzio – but fortunately even in those days celebrity had become a strong selling-point, and American War Correspondents were national names. Hollywood made films about them, wearing trench coats and Holding the Front Page and being gallant. Before the pleasantly businesslike Matron I dropped the famous names that were sleeping on our floor – though excluded Packard, just in case the word had got round. When I later drove triumphantly across to the hospital reception, there waited half-a-dozen jolly off-duty nurses and Red Cross girls evidently quite ready to raise our spirits and briefly escape their endless and harrowing lines of casualties.

They piled happily into the jeep and we returned to our Mess, to find it tidily rearranged, bottles opened expectantly – and the tough swaggering Correspondents surprisingly shy. We passed an excellent evening, discussed everything except the war, drank everything available, and much appreciated the company of pleasant young women in their fatigues and make-up who had made an effort to become glowing replicas of peacetime party-goers. During the evening the spasmodic shelling was so commonplace it hardly interrupted conversation. Packard was on his best behaviour, being suave in a world-weary WarCo way. You would never have guessed.

We planned future escapes for them, said our farewells affectionately, and I drove them back to the 95th Evac . . . where in stunned horror we confronted havoc and disaster. A damaged Luftwaffe aircraft about to crash-land had jettisoned five anti-personnel bombs across the hospital's tented lines. These killed three nurses and a Red Cross girl in their Mess tent, along with 22 staff and patients, and wounded 60 others. The place became known as Hell's Half Acre.

THEY DIED WITHOUT ANYONE EVEN KNOWING
THEIR NAMES . . .

Anzio and Cassino were planned as the twin military pinnacles of our Italian campaign; instead they became tragic examples of Allied Generalship at its most disastrous.

After the US VI Corps had enjoyed a classic and almost uncontested assault landing on the Anzio beaches, General Lucas decided that his 50,000 men – plus me – should dig-in and wait indefinitely for reinforcements, before considering any attack. This condemned us to a probable Dunkirk, or at best a struggle for survival amid the dead hopes of a Roman liberation. The Anzio landing had been intended to end the Cassino deadlock but instead of riding gallantly to their rescue, we now hoped someone would come and rescue *us*.

At the other end of this comatose Allied pincer movement, an even more disastrous international decision was taken by Field Marshal Alexander, supported by Generals Freyberg and Clark. In four hours, 239 heavy and medium bombers of Major General Nathan F. Twining's Mediterranean Allied Strategic Air Force dropped 453½ tons of bombs on the glorious Benedictine monastery of Monte Cassino. Each Flying Fortress carried twelve 500lb demolition bombs.

For 1400 years this mother of all monasteries, one of Christianity's largest and most sacred sites, stood proudly amid the wild peaks of the Abruzzi; then, in a few explosive hours, we reduced it to rubble.

After the bombing the US Army Air Support Group reported enthusiastically, 'A remarkable spectacle for the many ground observers who were able to see that precision bombing is a fact, not merely an expression.'

Some 230 Italian civilians died following this 'precision', but no Monks and no Germans. At the same time the Allies received an early but bitter taste of American 'friendly fire' which was to become notorious in later wars: the Eighth Army commander lost his caravan headquarters three miles from Cassino, and the French Corps HQ twelve miles away was heavily bombed. The 4th Indian Division suffered 25 Punjabi casualties. Mark Clark was in his command post seventeen miles away when sixteen bombs exploded nearby – and he was the General who agreed to the bombing. They all, I believe, had a vehement 'expression' for the spectacle . . .

The destruction of the Abbey was accepted as the supreme example of the failure of Allied strategy in Italy – so next day it was bombed again, to try and prevent the enemy using its ruins as strongpoints. Fifty-nine Marauder fighter-bombers flying from Sardinia dropped another 23 tons of bombs – or two-thirds of General Freyberg's original request.

No one ever discovered why the total bomb-load hitting the Abbey had escalated almost 300 times . . . Was it perhaps the US Strategic Air Force attempting to show a vast but unusual audience what it could do?

The world saw, all right. The Allies reaped no military benefit – except the applause and cheers of soldiers fighting for their lives on the slopes below the monastery and its all-seeing eyes. Those who were not there but watched the films saw it as an act of barbarism to be deplored by the rest of the world.

The bombing had been requested by Lieutenant General Sir Bernard Freyberg VC, whose New Zealand Corps, with the 4th Indian Division and the 1st Battalion of the Royal Sussex, had suffered heavily at the hands of the entrenched 1st Parachute Division. A man of action and courage, but limited intellect, Freyberg was convinced that despite denials the enemy was using the monastery as an artillery OP controlling fire against Kiwis bravely attempting an impossible assault on an almost impregnable enemy. He insisted upon the elimination of this ancient site of art and learning, and was supported by Brigadier H. W. Dimoline, an artillery officer then commanding the Indian Division which after the bombing would make the assault on Monastery Hill.

The belief among fighting troops that the monastery was occupied by Paras was almost certainly not true, though the vast and holy shrine did form a vital component of the Germans' Gustav defence line overlooking the Liri Valley; and Generaloberst Eberhard von Mackensen, Prussian aristocrat commanding the Fourteenth Army, had allowed his paratroops to occupy natural caves in the hill below the foundations of the Abbey, and positions within 50 feet of its walls.

The Abbey alone covered more than seven acres, its agreed 300-metre protected zone 80 acres. Within the sanctuary of that neutral zone the Germans had a cave in which they stored munitions, another used as a command post, and several machine gun positions.

The Roman Catholic world was aghast when what was seen as brutal vandalism gave the Nazi Propaganda Minister Dr Goebbels a major victory. Fortunately the Germans had transferred 15 trucks full of the monastery's treasures and books to the safety of the Vatican. Also, eighteen cases of its jewellery and bronzes had gone directly to Germany as a 51st birthday present for Marshal Goering from the Hermann Goering Division – a different sort of safety. This worked, in a way. At the end of the war fifteen cases were found by Americans in a salt mine near Alt-Aussee in Austria. They had suffered only minor damage.

The terrible decision – to bomb, or not to bomb – was crystallised by Field Marshal Alexander who said, 'Commanders, if faced by the choice between risking a single soldier's life or destroying a work of art – even a religious symbol – can make only one decision.' His Chief of Staff, General Sir John Harding, explained, 'Field Marshal Alexander regrets very much that the monastery should be destroyed, but he sees no other choice.' General Eisenhower, the Supreme Allied Commander, supported them: 'If we have to choose between destroying a famous building and sacrificing our own men, then our men's lives count infinitely more – and the buildings must go . . . nothing can stand against the argument of military necessity.'

In London, Sir Harold Nicolson, author and wartime Junior Minister, declared he would rather his son Nigel should die than the monastery be destroyed. 'Works of art are irreplaceable,' he said. 'Human lives are replaceable.' As a soldier in the battle, I must say I never saw it *quite* that way.

He did not then know that his son was fighting at Cassino as a Captain in the Grenadier Guards, and would survive to write books about General Montgomery and Field Marshal Alexander.

On February 14 after weeks of defeat, the USAAF had been called in to drop leaflets on the Abbey addressed to *Amici Italiani* and warning monks and civilians to leave before an air attack. Next day the bombers flew-in . . . and the Fifth Army planned to walk-in the day after. Unfortunately no one appreciated the tenacity of the Paras, who came out fighting with fanatical fury. Our infantry, when it could reach them, found they were still manning

Left: An enemy 15cm armoured Infantry Howitzer in firing position amid the ruins of Carroceto.

Below: Captured American troops are marched through Rome, under armed guard.

Right: Other German soldiers are less dominant. Held at gunpoint after capture by New Zealand troops during the Battle of Cassino.

Above: On the road to Rome an Italian cyclist voices his opinion of the German Army – by then safely disarmed and marching to the stockade.

Right: Taking pictures in a POW camp, one face seemed to me to symbolize the end of Teutonic dreams of conquest. I called this portrait 'The Master Race'. Next to that tragic figure, a young German POW appreciated that, for him at least, the war was over.

Along the beach Sergeant J. Huggett had also just got ashore. Ahead of him some Commandos were holding a small promontory against heavy German counter-attacks. Huggett, tall and game, set off up the hill to get pictures of the action. Near the top an angry voice ordered, 'This way! *This* way!' It was the Commando officer.

'You took your bloody time, Sergeant,' he shouted. 'Where the hell are your men?' Huggett admitted that he had come alone, to get pictures. '*What?*' cried the officer, after an emotional silence, 'I called for reinforcements, not a fucking photographer.'

One understands exactly how he felt; there are times when you just don't want your picture taken – even though it may well be your last . . .

The Luftwaffe flew in close-support for Kesselring's 15 divisions; for the first time we were outnumbered and clinging-on desperately. After two days the landing was going so badly that the Allied Commander, the American General Mark Clark, prepared plans for re-embarkation. He seemed ready to pack up and go home. His Army had only one escape route – by sea. It was unnerving to learn that our own Commander had even *considered* running back to the ships and sailing away.

He was eventually discouraged by tougher minds among senior American and British officers like Rear Admiral Tom Troubridge who could see that an attempted re-embarkation on beaches dominated by German artillery in the overlooking hills would be a massacre. They bullied and finally persuaded him against the possibility of retreat, but for indecisive days the Allies faced their first major defeat.

The crisis on the beaches followed a flawed invasion plan drawn up by inexperienced officers in which two of our three assault divisions had been given defensive missions. The third, the 46th Division, carried the lone offensive role – but was landed too far from Salerno for its execution. The result was a desperate battle to establish the beachhead by three separate and un-cooperating forces. There was also a seven-mile gap between our X Corps and the US VI Corps. No wonder General Clark despaired.

Back at AFHQ Eisenhower had heard that his friend was plan-ning re-embarkation, and worried that he might have lost his nerve. He told his USN ADC that Clark should show the spirit of a naval Captain and if necessary, go down with his ship. This seemed unlikely.

One echo of the desperation on the beaches survives in Salerno today: in a tidy but little-visited monumental garden in town stands a very small memorial. You need to crouch down to read its inscription. Few passers-by would notice its anguished cry – the thoughts and reactions of the men of the American 45th Infantry Division which put ashore two regimental combat teams under Major General Troy Middleton. Their scorn and bitterness is conveyed by two quotations inscribed on this stone, this memory of desperation.

General Mark Clark US Fifth Army Commander: *'Prepare to evacuate the beach.'* Underneath, the words of his subordinate, Major General Middleton: *'Leave the water and the ammo on the beach. The 45th Division is here to stay.'*

It is rare indeed for a division to castigate publicly its Army Commander for considering sailing away from the battle. Rarer still, President Roosevelt later awarded Clark the Distinguished Service Cross for gallantry at Salerno.

Lieutenant General Mark W. Clark – Wayne to his friends – graduated from West Point in 1917, 109th in a class of 135, and was afterwards a Captain for 16 years. His career took-off with the war and the friendship of General Eisenhower, with whom he their strongpoints while our supporting tanks were unable to move through rain-filled bomb craters. The Germans were skilled at reconstruction; as roofs fell in and walls collapsed, survivors used the readily available broken stone to strengthen their underground bunkers. The bombing had made our attacks more hazardous and created anti-tank obstacles against our own Army.

In an unusual tribute to an enemy, Field Marshal Alexander explained the Allies' latest failure to the Chief of the Imperial General Staff: 'It seemed to me inconceivable that any troops should be left alive after eight hours of such terrific hammering. Unfortunately we are fighting the best soldiers in the world – what men! I doubt if there are any other troops who could have stood up to the bombing and then gone on fighting with the ferocity they have.' After eight days Alexander called-off that offensive.

The bombing Freyberg had insisted upon at least brought the two opposing Army Commanders together: the Catholic General Mark Clark, and von Mackensen who merely said, 'The idiots – they've done it after all!' Both deplored the attack.

The air attack had been a failure. It had produced spectacular destruction but had not broken the morale of the defenders. It merely destroyed a monastery. Even in clear skies and without opposition, it was so inaccurate that most bombs missed the Abbey altogether, and the remainder were resisted by medieval walls 10-feet thick. Our artillery was more accurate; yet after a two-hour bombardment by 900 guns, when the Allies attacked again they were unsuccessful. Each head-on infantry assault on that 1700-foot mountainside followed the last attack identically so, as General von Mackensen explained, our tactics held no surprises for his men. They turned the ruins into a fortress and withstood all attacks for another three months.

The manpower situation on the Cassino front grew desperate when the repeated assaults of Alexander and Clark frittered away our strength piecemeal, squandering fine divisions in isolated and inadequately supported attacks. In such a desperate situation it was curious that the British troops of McCreary and the Kiwis of Freyberg were sometimes left unused by General Clark. He was becoming paranoid about Allies who had to deal with the problem of *not* being American and, even worse, of often being successful and well led. He described the Cassino fighting as 'the most gruelling, the most harassing and in one aspect the most tragic phase of the war in Italy'. Certainly many men died from poor leadership.

Again and again the Fifth Army attacked the most powerful defensive position in Italy, held by the Wehrmacht's finest troops. Finally on May 11 another Allied offensive attempted for the first time to outflank Cassino. It cost the Poles 860 dead and 3,000 wounded. Despite losses they fought their way to the north of Cassino, and a week later cleared Cassino town. After the battle 900 German corpses were recovered.

The Paras' magnificent defence of their mountaintop had grown manic. Even when Kesselring agreed a retreat some men who had been there for months refused to leave, preferring to fight to the end – and take a few more Allied soldiers with them. When their surviving comrades finally walked out of the ruins voluntarily and withdrew, they stayed behind in the battered fortress and fought their last brave battle into oblivion.

On May 18 the red and white standard of the Poles flew over Monastery Hill. First to enter the gutted monastery: a platoon of Uhlans of the Podolski Lancers.

There can be no bright side to this military tragedy – except to know that perhaps the international outrage which followed our bombing of Monte Cassino may in some way have helped to spare Rome an even worse fate . . .

* * *

Anzio had brought back to the Italian battlefields the trench warfare of the First World War. It became a muddy sodden struggle complete with duckboards, mortars and patrols into no-man's-land. Sometimes even hand-to-hand fighting through the dreaded wadis north of the Padiglione woods and the Flyover, where our first carefree drive towards Rome had stopped abruptly. We were enduring another Somme in the era of blitzkrieg and rockets.

By the beginning of February '44 the Germans had amassed well over 90,000 troops in a tight ring around Anzio. We were now defensive, and clinging on. Passing Hitler's orders down the line, Field Marshal Kesselring ordered Generaloberst von Mackensen's Fourteenth Army to annihilate the beachhead. To push us back into the sea he called-up 17 battalions of infantry supported by 144 long-range artillery guns, howitzers and rocket launchers. There were also 169 anti-aircraft guns and the tank battalions of the 26th Panzer Division, supported by two further battle groups of infantry, 20 Tiger and 25 Mk III tanks, 25 assault guns – and doubtless much more. The counter-attack General Lucas expected as he stepped ashore all those bloody weeks ago was finally coming, while we marked time until the enemy was ready.

Casualties in that kind of static trench warfare would average several hundred a day, but could only be replaced by some 500 men a day. Reinforcements would arrive to be pushed into the Line and perhaps captured or killed within hours. In the terrible artillery barrages both sides laid down, men would disappear without trace. They often died without anyone even knowing their names.

This war had become so bitter and despairing that, in another horrible echo of the Great War trenches, shocked soldiers would mutilate themselves in an effort to avoid the battle – which at times promised almost certain death.

In the long casualty lists both sides issued, Missing In Action often meant Captured and Imprisoned. That's what relatives hoped. Sometimes it could mean Deserted. Amid the screaming horror of the battlefield even the bravest men could reach their limits of courage and endurance, when it seemed easier to stop struggling, give up, and raise your hands.

German treatment of prisoners was usually correct, as was ours, but every would-be prisoner had to survive those first confused minutes of surrender amid the destruction of bullets and shells, when instinct called for self-survival and escape.

The Germans often marched prisoners through the streets of Rome to show the populace and the newspapers at home who seemed to be winning. We did not display prisoners as they were despatched through the lines; at Anzio they were quickly sent aboard the chain of supply LSTs, back to Naples. We had no room for them on the bridgehead.

I went to take some pictures of POWs passing through a cage at Nettuno, on their way back to a prison camp in the South. One gaunt skeletal German caught my eye. Beneath his steel helmet was a sunken lined face. Expressionless, unemotional, silent and withdrawn, he seemed old and beaten, and to me symbolised the end of Teutonic dreams of conquest. I afterwards captioned my pictures, 'The Master Race'. I later saw these pictures on magazine covers from around the world.

As I was lining-up a final picture of him I suddenly realised that this middle-aged soldier standing before me . . . had started to *cry*, silently. He was weeping. I did not know why: Humiliation? Exhaustion? Apprehension?

Whatever the reason, his distress was pitiful, so I stopped taking pictures and moved away. I never saw him again. I hope he survived his defeat.

Next to him in my album is another picture taken that

morning of the young boy soldier who stood with him, grinning delightedly at the end of his military career. He knew he would soon be heading for home, to start his life again.

They stood together in that mournful place: the indelibly tragic and cheerful faces of The Master Race.

One morning the front between Carroceto and Campoleone was quiet and peaceful. This was a bad sign – it usually meant something dreadful was about to happen. Men stared watchfully into the menacing, brooding distance. Silence.

The curtain-raiser – not at all dreadful, at first – was the arrival of a hundred sheep scampering towards our lines across no-man's-land. Untroubled by the RSPCA vote, the enemy were using them as mine detectors – so their intention to attack was obvious. Sheep that survived were then hit by a massive artillery barrage, followed by a steady German advance across no-man's-land towards the lines of the Irish Guards.

Their infantrymen moved bravely through terrifying Irish machine gun fire, shouting *'Gott mit uns.'* The Irish Guards instantly gave them the opportunity of discovering whether that was true, or not. They fired until their ammunition ran out, then desperately attacked the surprised enemy with bare fists before escaping into the wadis. You can only pull a courageous trick like that once . . .

In the caves along the bays of Buonriposo Ridge the men of the 2nd Battalion US 157th Regiment were surrounded by enemy positions. Not even tanks could reach them by road or track. They had to be supplied by air drops. The only source of water for their foremost company was a stream running red with the blood of several dead Germans. As days passed that water was boiled – and *drunk* by parched soldiers.

Our casualties were dreadful: the Scots Guards had four commanding officers in the first three weeks of fighting. The British lst Division, which had brought me to Anzio, lost 1600 men in a few days. In the first two weeks their Rifle Battalions lost half their strength and most of their officers, some who had also been losers – I was saddened to remember – at shipboard poker . . .

The gallant commando-style US Rangers sent 767 men into one attack. Six returned. All officers of B and C Companies of the King's Shropshire Light Infantry were casualties, so company sergeant majors took over – and were killed in their turn.

In pushing us back from Carroceto, the Panzer Grenadiers captured a gully and found it full of British dead. The corpse of one British soldier was being eaten by three starving pigs. The Grenadiers shot the pigs and buried the soldier.

Most daunting threats of all were the massed Tiger tanks bearing down upon Allied positions – like some monstrous Red Army parade through Moscow. It is hard to envisage 57 tons until you see them in motion, coming towards you. Squadrons of Tigers were thrown into the attack and came bonging along like so many church steeples as our artillery got their range and scored hits with armour-piercing shells.

For Germans the worst moment must have been when several hundred Allied aircraft, many of them Wellingtons, risked close support and dropped 1,000 tons of bombs across their lines. Four days of such battles cost the Allies about 5,000 men, the Germans probably more. The 2nd Sherwood Foresters suffered the dreadful honour of having the largest percentage of fatalities of any British battalion on the bridgehead: 100 per cent of their men, and 200 per cent of their officers.

The inevitable reward for such a climax with its terrible toll was stalemate, for a little while. Should you manage to survive this battle of the Titans, you began to feel immortal . . . though not for long.

Amid the wretched bloody squalor, constant rain flooded fox-holes. A new trench would slowly fill with water before the digger could move in. Some foxholes would be only 50 feet from the German positions, so when troops were not trying to kill each other, they could at least shout at each other. Shallow graves had to be dug again every night, for sweeping floodwater would wash away the rough crosses made from ration boxes, along with the earth from the top of the graves. Sometimes a dangling arm or a leg would appear.

Attempting to film such a warfront was even more difficult than I had expected. First of all, not even our own side was always pleased to see us. This was a new experience – we were usually a much-appreciated diversion. Army Film Unit was painted on the front of my jeep, and following any truck on the road I would usually be treated to that old British Movietone News theme chanted by squaddies in the back, all winding their im-aginary cameras at me, as seen at the end of pre-war cinema newsreels.

This sudden lack of welcome was not personal and, in trench warfare, easily understood: movement brought shells. Even the Allied Commander, Field Marshal Alexander upset some of his American units. A brave soldier with DSO and MC from the Great War, Alex did visit his men in the front lines – unlike some Generals – but at Anzio he excited a new reaction. German artillery observation posts up in the Alban Hills missed nothing, and US troops complained that 'the guy in the Red Hat' was attracting shells. They urged him to prove his bravery elsewhere. Everyone was within range in Anzio, but this was an unusual complaint for the impeccable and courteous Field Marshal to handle.

I had certainly not been elevated to the red-tab realm, but did represent Movement in the lines, to which enemy OPs would react, unfortunately sometimes after I had taken my pictures, and gone.

I was more welcome at night-time – but then could rarely get pictures. Anyhow, social calls were not encouraged and it was always strange to be struggling to get such an invitation. Reaching the front even in daylight was a long, slow and dangerous business, and always felt like moving towards death.

Like most major conflicts today Anzio became a war of artillery, which controlled the occasional surges of infantry. The terrain was usually unsuitable for tanks which ground deep into the mud. The enemy was too close for regular air support, so distant big guns controlled and intimidated the wretched infantrymen.

On one normally noisy day in May the Navy HQ on the harbourside decided to count the number of heavy shells coming over to hit shipping or whatever in Anzio harbour, just below our villa. They clocked 609 in one day – that's more than one every minute in a 10-hour working day – almost too fast to count your blessings. You can see why we got the Anzio Twitch.

Despite that constant bombardment, the port continued to unload four LSTs and three LCIs simultaneously and, out at sea, four 10,000-ton Liberty ships every ten days. These were serviced by a busy fleet of more than 500 LCTs and DUKWs. The turnover of our little fishing village then ranked seventh among the great ports of the world.

Supplies and ammo arrived aboard LSTs ready-loaded on fleets of six-wheeled trucks. Upon docking these would roar down the ramps, off the quayside and away, flat out, while empty trucks bounced back on board to fill their places, fast. This reduced unloading time from a day, to an hour. Nobody hung around that harbour.

Yet should you pause to listen (not advisable) it was always the same. First you'd hear a distant, almost discreet cough, deep behind enemy lines. Then a slight pause during which you knew the shell was heading your way. The bone-shaking *crump* would be a relief – that one at least did not have your name on it. The sound would swiftly catch-up and echo into the distance like a tube-train racing away down its long dark tunnel.

Then you listened for the next one . . .

I'M AFRAID WE'RE NOT QUITE READY FOR YOU YET . . .

Long rows of casualties on stretchers and in varying degrees of distress would be lined-up on the Anzio quayside under whatever cover there was, waiting for the next LST returning to Naples. They could do nothing but lie and listen to Annie, poor chaps. Such a distressing collection of misery was not an encouraging introduction to the bridgehead for the apprehensive reinforcements disembarking from LSTs to fill their places in the front line. With a few awkward words, they walked stiffly – perhaps even a little enviously – past stretcher-cases bound for some distant peaceful hospital in Sorrento, while they headed towards the battlefront.

The port's regular tormentors were two huge 280mm railway guns – the 215-ton Anzio Annie and Anzio Express – biggest guns fired during the entire war. The Germans, who do not have the light touch, called these ponderous monsters Leopold and Robert. They operated from the Nemi tunnel on a branch route connecting with the Rome-Naples main line. Each needed a team of ten men and could fire a shell weighing a quarter of a ton more than 20 miles – or with rocket assistance, an inaccurate but frightening 53 miles. It took up to ten hours to prepare a gun to start firing one shell every five minutes. They were afterwards shunted back into their tunnel, away from our bombers.

Both could have been neutralized, of course, if the nearby railway lines had been bombed. Seems nobody thought of that . . .

After the breakout from the bridgehead the Anzio Express was found damaged in its home tunnel at Nemi, but beyond salvage – probably due to German demolition. Anzio Annie escaped, but was captured later in Civitavecchia, north of Rome, and sent back to the United States through the port of Naples, with enormous difficulty. That biggest war trophy finally came to rest in a railway siding at the Aberdeen Proving Ground in Maryland as the showpiece of the US Army Ordnance Museum.

Having saturated us with high explosives, the Germans began to fire propaganda leaflets as well. These proclaimed what was a terrible truth: that Anzio was the biggest and best prison camp in the world – because the prisoners were self-supporting.

Others showed a soldier's wife back in England preparing for bed while in the background an American master sergeant undresses purposefully. 'What English girl could refuse these handsome men from the wide open spaces?' asked the leaflet.

These would arrive as a snowstorm, and be made welcome; the troops' reaction was to tear-off the text and use the girl as a pin-up. They always seemed to me quaint and unerotic – like faded Victorian pornography with little impact – though were more acceptable than high explosives.

Americans always seemed to us rather lavish in their distribution of medals – indeed some were handed out automatically, like the Purple Heart which seemed to go to every man checked into a field hospital, however prosaic his complaint.

US Army Public Relations had taken over the villa next to ours for War Correspondents. On one bad morning several 500lb Luftwaffe bombs hit the area. In a panic the Press – including Ernie Pyle, a famous American Correspondent – took-off for the cellars, scrambling downstairs so fast that some tumbled and hurt themselves. As they left hospital after treatment for various bruises and sprains they were handed their Purple Heart medals. Then they wore them. Now that *did* call for courage.

Before he returned to the US from the catacombs of Nettuno, Major General Lucas was awarded a Silver Star for gallantry at Anzio, and a Distinguished Service Medal as VI Corps Commander – though he did not even *try* to get to Rome. The US Navy awarded him their Distinguished Service Medal for his role in the landing – though it seemed he did nothing, and risked nothing. His Commanding General Mark Clark, who was no coward, had a magnificent fruit-salad of medals too humorous to mention.

Until the bridgehead, Anzio's only claim to fame had been as the birthplace of the Roman Emperor Nero. He seems to have been the only person who ever much liked the place.

I was reading *Agony At Anzio* by the American author William Breuer. He wrote that an ornate palace had been built for 'the fun-loving Emperor Nero'. This seemed rather like calling Adolf Hitler 'roguish'. Later when describing the breakout from the Anzio Bridgehead, 'General Clark felt a strange thrill surge through his being.' Hmm.

Another book, *The Battle for Rome,* recalled attempts by American units to distract the enemy at Anzio by small raids along the coast, behind their lines. The author wrote enthusiastically about one daring amphibious landing near La Spezia: 'It was very successful – but the whole team was captured and shot.'

A success like that can quite spoil your day.

* * *

The Germans unleashed upon our shipping early secret weapons which in 1944 lifted the curtain on robot warfare – glider-bombs controlled by the plane which fired them were launched with frightening success. The battleship *Warspite* was hit, and the US cruisers *Savannah* and *Philadelphia*. The cruiser *Penelope* was sunk, but by a submarine. The cruiser *Spartan* followed them into the deep, along with various Liberty ships and minesweepers, and the hospital ship *St David* which was lying out to sea fully illuminated, in accordance with the Geneva Convention.

From our terrace we watched with horror as these early V-bombs sank ship after ship. They seemed invincible. The great crimson glare across the night sky as a Liberty ship loaded with ammunition and petrol exploded was heart-stopping.

They introduced Goliath, a small remote-controlled tank carrying 800lbs of explosives. Fortunately he was easily distracted by mud, or neutralised by unfriendly fire. They launched a tiny one-man submarine which lay in wait for our nightly convoys of supply ships coming in from Naples. We began to feel that Superman was on their side – along with Buck Rogers, and Flash Gordon.

So more than a quarter of a million men were locked in a brutal struggle for a small patch of the sodden plains of the Pontine marshes. It was not an easy place in which to stay alive.

After one battle the Irish Guards' historian wrote, 'The silent courage of maimed, battered, bleeding Irish Guardsmen lying in some muddy ditch was a living monument to the strength of the human will in the depths of human misery. A man drained of blood gets very cold, and there is not much a man with a shattered thigh can do for himself. A man whose chest has been torn to ribbons by shell splinters would like to be moved out of the barrage – but no one said anything, no one asked for anything. They just smiled painfully when someone put a blanket over them, or gave them a drink of water and a cigarette.'

In field hospitals the British and US medical services struggled desperately to cope with the multitude of wounded and dying men. They worked on the defiant principle that, 'There's no such thing as a corpse, until the funeral.' When a soldier was wounded, it took on average seven hours to get him to the operating table at Anzio, but often very much longer. Sometimes he had to wait until night for collection when, between flares, he could be manhandled back to a sickbay, somewhere.

One gravely-injured young officer at a field hospital had been waiting all day on a stretcher and, as a doctor hurried by, asked quietly if his injuries could be treated. The doctor saw instantly that there was no hope for him, so said gently, 'I'm afraid we're not quite ready for you yet.' The young officer nodded. 'I understand,' he said, and closed his eyes.

In wartime brilliant fragments of courage and nobility can pass by, unnoticed; so Rest In Peace, young brother-officer. You had 60 years of life taken from you in the sad, dreadful place that was Anzio. You are not forgotten by those who marched with you.

YOU SHOULD HAVE HEARD HIM
SCREAMING . . .

Churchill, the driving-force behind the ill-fated bridge-head, believed an amphibious landing behind German lines would break the deadlock at Monte Cassino, but tragically all it produced was another deadlock further north, and unhappy echoes of his Dardanelles disaster. Unfortunately we were then commanded by two American Generals – Clark and Lucas – who neither understood nor liked their more experienced British Allies, and had little faith in the operation.

When Lucas's inertia at Anzio left us surrounded and besieged for months, Churchill was livid. 'I had hoped we were hurling a wildcat onto the shore' he said, 'but all we got was a stranded whale.' He was even more furious when he learned there were 18,000 vehicles on our tiny bridgehead. 'Highly organised insanity,' he said, 'and they were stopped after twelve miles.' That was generous. They only got *seven* miles inland. The Prime Minister's appreciation: 'We must have a great superiority of chauffeurs . . .'

Even during the planning for *Shingle* he had been unhappy about the deep-seated American conviction that, 'Two legs bad – four wheels good'. He reminded Field Marshal Alexander caustically, 'I do hope that when you have landed this great quantity of lorries and cannon, you will find room for a *few* foot-soldiers – if only to guard the lorries.'

Fortunately his Chief Military Deputy, General Sir Hasting Ismay, was wise enough not to let him know that some of the first crates ashore at Anzio were found to contain harmoniums and hymn books . . .

After a disastrous month of indecision and inaction Alexander finally determined that Lucas must go, to widespread relief. Major General Gerald Templer summed him up: 'He had no qualities of any sort as a Commander – the antithesis of everything a fighting soldier and General ought to be.' My memory of him is of a quiet old scoutmaster being helped into layers of coats. He was not an inspiring Commander, and died soon after the war while ballroom dancing.

His place at Anzio was taken by a tough officer in the flamboyant Patton mould, Major General Lucian K. Truscott III, who added a white scarf to the US Generals' approved gear of pearl-handled revolvers and shiny helmet.

Another American General with a disparaging view of the British Army arrived to command the impressive US 1st Armoured Division. Major General Ernest N. Harmon, a skilled and brave officer, soon changed his opinion.

He had gone to the front to investigate a hold-up on the Sherwood Foresters' sector, and afterwards wrote, 'I had never seen so many dead men in one place. They lay so close together I had to step with care. I shouted for the Commanding Officer. From a foxhole there arose a mud-covered Corporal with a handlebar moustache. He was the highest-ranking officer still alive. He stood stiffly to attention. 'How is it going?' I asked. 'Well sir,' the Corporal said, 'there were 116 of us when we first came up and there are sixteen of us left. We were ordered to hold out until sundown and I think, with a little good fortune, we can manage to do so.'

General Harmon added, 'My great respect for the stubbornness and fighting ability of the British enlisted man was born that afternoon.'

In every battle there comes a moment when both sides are suddenly aware that bravery is no longer enough. They can struggle no more. On the beachhead that came after our great air attack on March 2, which stunned the enemy with its overwhelming power. It seemed as though the Germans had gambled everything they had to achieve Hitler's order: 'Throw them into the sea, and drown them.'

They now had nothing left to give. Their military reputation, their plans for the future, their reserves of men and materials, everything had been committed at Anzio, but still without victory. From now on the splendid Wehrmacht, forged with pride and skill and courage, could no longer be sure to sweep all before it. The world now saw it could be beaten. Never again would Germans be able to send their men into the attack inspired by the certainty of ultimate conquest.

The 3rd Panzer Grenadiers had arrived as reinforcements from Stalingrad and when captured the tough veterans told us that Anzio was far worse than the Russian front. We took a strange satisfaction in that. At least we were their worst enemy, in the worst place.

At Anzio we had just managed to fight off three attempts to push us back into the Tyrrhenian. We suffered 43,000 casualties plus another 44,000 hospitalised for various reasons. The Germans lost about 40,000. They had gained some ground – but our backs were still a few miles from the sea and we believed we had seen their last throw.

Kesselring had frustrated the bridgehead, but could not destroy it. After we had resisted his third major attack it became apparent that the two armies had fought themselves to a standstill, and were shattered. This time it was unlikely there would be a recovery. Kesselring, who had become an expert at *not* telling Hitler what Hitler did not wish to hear, had not got to be a Field Marshal without becoming a smart tactician. He sent his Chief of Staff General Siegfried Westphal to Berchtesgaden to tell the Führer the unhappy news, rather than going himself.

During three anxious hours Westphal explained that although their forces in Italy could still fight defensively, Army Group 'C' was no longer capable of taking the offensive. The armies had been shattered by five years of war, and were now exhausted.

Such a defensive sit-rep would normally have produced a frenzy of shouting or ice-cold fury from the Führer, to which Generals had little answer. This time however the uncomfortable news was received calmly. Afterwards the surprised guardians of the inner sanctum who softened bad news for the Führer, Field Marshal Keitel and Generaloberst Jodl, told Westphal, 'You were lucky. If we old fools had said even half as much, the Führer would have had us hung.' (Fourteen months' later that cautious couple, the Field Marshal and the General representing their High Command, signed the Unconditional Surrender of the German forces which ended the war).

Hitler had further surprised them by ordering a cross-section of 20 front-line officers of various ranks to be flown from the Italian front to his mountaintop retreat, the Berghof, to be questioned about the fighting at Anzio – a new and constructive reaction from a Dictator who never listened to his Generals.

As Hitler had for once heard the straight truth, Kesselring was able to call-off his despairing last-ditch attack planned for March 1 '44. His attempts to eliminate the bridgehead without adequate

Left: After the Anzio landing, I could see that General Lucas, Commander of the US VI Corps, was not marching on Rome and had no intention of attacking anyone, anywhere, so I took over a villa on the coast road overlooking the port.

Below: . . . and almost unchanged today.

Above: AFPU's new HQs seemed tough enough to resist constant shelling. Indeed it turned out to be a lucky villa . . .

Left: From our sitting room we could get all the shellfire pictures we wanted, without leaving home . . .

Right: Field Marshall Alexander, Supreme Commander, finally fired General Lucas and replaced him with the fire-eating General Lucien K. Truscott III. Front Line fashions for Generals and above: Alexander wears a leather bomber jacket over jodhpurs and boots, and what US troops called his 'red hat'. Truscott has the traditional American General's gear of shiny helmet, leather jacket, but completes his ensemble with *gloves* . . .

Left: Lieut. Peter Hopkinson and I set off to see if we could break-out of the Bridgehead through the German lines to the south, and reach Naples with our photographic scoop. On a temporary bridge we ran into a couple of locals returning home – fortunately *not* the German army.

Right: General Mark Clark was a vain man who loved publicity and dreamed of liberating Rome – preferably on his own. For this shot with Major General Keyes, and the following pictures, Mark Clark allowed Kesselring's two armies to escape. This extended the war by a year and cost us countless casualties.

Above left and right: My picture of Mark Clark arriving at the Capitol in Rome went around the world . . . as did the shot of the first serious Union Jack to fly in Rome, on Liberation Day.

Below: General Clark had a personal PR staff of some 50, and his permanent cameraman followed him everywhere. He would only allow photographs from his *left* side, as his tame photographer knew well.

Above: In Rome I went to the home of some friends on the Corso Umberto for top-shots of the Fifth Army arriving in the Capital. Some of the crowd were applauding the first jeeps, but others had spotted my team on the balcony and were applauding *us!*

Above: I enjoyed the blissful acceptance of one uniformed American who was kissed from both sides by happy ladies. I assumed he was some fortunate GI – but he turned out to be another Correspondent. It seemed unfair.

Above: "Rome Liberated Today" says the headline amid the handsome faces of celebrating Romans. They all looked like film stars to me.

Above: On the evening of Liberation Day 200,000 Romans gathered in St Peter's Square to be blessed by Pope Pius XII, who thanked both sides for sparing Rome the destruction of war.

Left: He spoke from the balcony of St Peter's, and was greeted by tears of joy and relief.

Right: AFPU's more intimate celebration was at the Grand Hotel, along with Captain John D. Ford, American censor, and Sergeant French, AFPU photographer.

Florence, symbol of Tuscan pride, was a small but satisfying victory. British troops accepted the glory that is Florence quite calmly and Michelangelo's David – the most famous statue in the world – did not rate a second glance . . .

Left: . . . nor did the 800-year-old Duomo.

Below: The Germans blew up all the beautiful bridges across the River Arno except the Ponte Vecchio, which was permitted to survive, but the palaces and stately buildings around both ends of that bridge were destroyed to slow our advance.

Right and far right: We found the heart of Florence around the Duomo was undamaged.

Right: I put a couple of cameramen with the special force that broke through to Villa Spellman, the Gestapo headquarters. It was locked and deserted – and its front door was certainly *not* one of those that could be kicked in!

Below left: I requisitioned the Villa Paradisino, on the outskirts of Florence. It was owned by Ludovico Daneo and his vivacious Russian wife Patsya, here with their mandatory Alsatian and Lieuts. Groom and Craig.

Below right: The entrance to the Villa Paradisino is hardly changed after 60 years . . .

air support had finally failed, and the Tenth and Fourteenth Armies went on the defensive. So, within months, did Germany.

The remarkable war machine and its nation of some seventy-eight million had once again challenged the rest of the world, and once again almost won. They left behind in their eighteen million goose-steps a worldwide death toll of 50 million – about the population of Britain.

This was the beginning of the end, the day the circus left town. Wiser strategists in the War Departments of London, Washington and Berlin got their first inkling that the invincible Wehrmacht was about to be beaten in Italy and then, surely, in the bigger battles for Russia, France and Germany soon to be fought.

The signs were already there in Russia with its endless supply of mute but obedient cannon fodder bringing the German defeat at Stalingrad. North Africa had been a resounding victory for the British armies, and the Royal Navy was finally defeating the U-boats in the Atlantic. Now, on the Third Front in Italy the bravest and most sturdy divisions of the German Army – the Parachutists, the Panzer Grenadiers, the SS – had come up against British County regiments with bucolic names like Sherwood Foresters, The North Irish Horse, Green Howards, King's Own Yorkshire Light Infantry, Gordon Highlanders, London Irish Rifles, The Scottish Horse and The Buffs . . . These country battalions were usually manned by part-time amateur officers and men 'in for the duration' but as in the Great War, were holding and then beating Germany's best.

They had been helped of course – sometimes magnificently – by American armoured divisions and Rangers, by the RAF and US Groups in the Allied Tactical Air Force which all-but drove the Luftwaffe from the skies, by the Polish Corps which finally stormed Monte Cassino, the French Corps with its brilliant General Juin, by the bravery of New Zealanders and South Africans, Indians and Canadians . . . Together they had faced two German armies led with masterly skill and fought them to a standstill, and disintegration. Now it was almost over – though on the fighting front, it never felt that way. It was hard to believe Jerry was almost beaten, again.

With the increasing German caution, and following three weeks of rain, our front line stabilised in the mud and became almost peaceful. This was when the wine store discovered in the cellars of Nettuno came to our support. The Italian air-raid signs pointing to the caves said *Al Ricovero,* meaning *To the Shelter,* but the troops thought some guy called Al had cornered the wine market and 'Going to Al's place' became a popular move.

One GI who had spent some time at Al's discovered on the way back to his Unit an old top hat in some ruins. With this on his head he paraded unsteadily but cheerfully around his Unit's positions, enjoying his audience until, sense of direction gone, he lurched towards the German lines.

His friends were silent, horrified by this suicidal display. The Panzer Grenadiers also watched his wobbly approach, but held their fire. When he finally reached them, they welcomed him, shook his hand, straightened his top hat, turned him round and pushed him back towards his own unit.

Even in the most bitter war there's an occasional happy incident.

During the stalemate, with armies quietly tensing and preparing to defend themselves if necessary, the front lines would sometimes fall silent, for any obvious movement was still fatal. It was then that the never-sleeping German artillery in the Alban Hills concentrated upon rear areas, the port and supply lines. Anzio Annie and the Anzio Express would emerge from their tunnels to terrify and kill. Their range could carry massive shells well past the supply ships unloading more than ten miles out to sea.

At dusk our fighter cover was withdrawn – the Go signal for enemy bombers. After our landing a fighter airstrip had been built outside Nettuno, but came under endless attack from enemy artillery and soon had to be abandoned.

Flares lit artillery targets after dark, when the front line was feverish. No one at Anzio ever thought of the night as friendly. The one exception might have been the BBC's cheery Correspondent and my good friend, the late Wynford Vaughan-Thomas who, planning to record a night-barrage of artillery, left his mike open one night and instead picked-up the exquisite nightingale of Anzio. As it sung its way through a million anxious nights, this happy bird won him more public acclaim than any of his other wartime assignments, which included bombing raids on Berlin.

At night no-man's-land sprung into grotesque action as supplies and ammo were brought in and wounded carried-out, until Very lights would suddenly illuminate the stark terrain and still movement across the dead country. As targets were spotted, shells would come hissing overhead and bullets crackle through the unnatural light. Tens of thousands of men were in that black wilderness somewhere but not one was visible, not one dared lift his head. Every living thing had gone to ground, under penalty of death. After dark, Anzio held its breath.

Even so, it was better to be wounded at night when between Very lights they could sometimes come and get you out. God help you if you were hit in the daytime; stretcher-bearers and medics were brave enough, but not suicidal. They knew snipers were waiting for any attempted rescue.

Night-time was when Sally and George would arrive to coax or frighten the men of the bridgehead. They were the voices of

Radio Rome, just up the road, and 11pm was their time to keep the Fifth Army company.

George specialised in soft menace and grizzly detail: 'Have you heard about Private Jones? He went on patrol and stepped on a schu mine. Nasty things, schu mines. All his guts were blown away – but he went on living for another twelve hours. You should have heard him screaming.' However much George's nasty routines were ridiculed, they could be unsettling.

Then there was Sally – there always was an Axis-Sally, even in the Pacific. The usual soft sexy seductive voice was aimed at unsettling troops and encouraging them to think of lower things during lonely nights. Of her type, she was a class act – though when she ultimately fell into Allied hands after the war was revealed as fat and unattractive.

In the summer of '44 Allied forces in Italy were weakened by the removal of the five US divisions required for the invasion of Southern France – enthusiastically championed by President Roosevelt and General Eisenhower but dismissed as irrelevant by Churchill. These landings were completely successful but though beachheads and battlefields were sunlit and elegant – Monte Carlo, St Tropez, Cannes – the invasion achieved little. Men and armour would surely have been more usefully employed – as Churchill urged – attending to our established wars in Italy or Normandy. However the Prime Minister had been reluctantly granted his unfortunate Anzio operation so now had to accept the Americans' conviction that the new French front would divert German troops and attention from Normandy. They were wrong, too.

We saw from our daily briefings at Corps HQ in the cellars of Nettuno that the main Fifth Army to the south had finally decided to stop its disastrous frontal attacks on Monte Cassino and was trying to outflank the enemy. It had also launched an attack north, towards us. With quiet desperation Lieutenant Peter Hopkinson and I decided that, as we were getting a trifle beachhead-crazy after months in the target area, this was the time to risk a private breakout and try to meet our rescuers half way.

Packing all our exposed film for delivery to the Developing Section in Naples, we drove quietly and hopefully out across the Mussolini Canal and into the Pontine marshes, watching for mines and snipers. Anzio's main fighting positions were now to the north, and the enemy should have withdrawn. It was eerily quiet.

After a few cautious miles with no enemy reaction we were stopped near Borgo Grappa by a broken bridge. As we wondered how to get the jeep round it we heard movement to the south, and took cover. It sounded reassuringly like an American patrol. Shouting, we attempted to persuade them not to fire at us. This was difficult because, apart from having the wrong accents, we also had the wrong silhouettes: we did not wear those globular helmets. They took a lot of convincing we were not goddam Krauts. Babbling English very loudly we eventually walked forward for the traditional link-up with men of the US 85th Division, to great excitement. It was the last of the bridgehead's 123 days.

Most of the US forces had also been withdrawn from this end of the bridgehead to reinforce the coming breakout, and General Mark Clark had come up to Anzio to star in the long-awaited link-up pictures. He arrived three hours late with 25 photographers and Correspondents in tow. The link-up then had to be restaged for the cameras with the General playing the lead and shaking hands with the men of the arriving 85th. For us, used to senior officers who were not expected to act, it was a new kind of actuality – as handled by Hollywood.

As soon as the bridge repairs could cope with a jeep, we left them to their orgy of flashes and congratulations and hurtled south on the hundred-mile drive to Naples, triumphantly carrying the first pictures of the relief of the bridgehead. We were not sure whether the enemy had withdrawn, and wondered if we might find ourselves behind some German rearguard which was not looking both ways. The road had certainly not been cleared for mines or booby traps, but we were too elated to worry.

We found ourselves alarming various American units by appearing excitedly in front of them, where the enemy should have been. Happily we raced on down the Naples road, through wartime normality. At one river we had to wait while they completed a bridge, with great good humour.

Then with the Relief of Anzio pictures the world was waiting for we pushed-on, every mile flat out, towards Naples and the transmission centre with our priceless scoop. As the first Bridgehead Boys we felt we should be bowing graciously and giving royal gestures to an admiring public. On the last mile down the Via Roma through the city centre towards our darkrooms, we were stopped by a jeepful of American Military Police in shiny helmets. We greeted them with cheerful fraternal modesty.

They gave us, not their congratulations, but a ticket for speeding.

The stern lecture that went with our ticket reminded me that reality on the battlefield was living and dying. A few miles away, it was observing somebody's peacetime restrictions.

Then there was the fire-eating Major General Ernie Harmon, commanding the US 1st Armoured Division at Anzio. When some of his front line men managed to get a rare four-day R&R pass to Naples, they sailed in and were soon arrested and jailed by MPs for wearing their uniforms improperly. Buttons were probably undone, too. Harmon's Chief of Staff had great difficulty in dissuading the crusty General from sending half his division down to Naples 'to clean up the city'. He would have found no shortage of volunteers. They say it takes at least seven supply men to keep one man fighting in the front line; certainly the MPs needed *someone* to give their tickets to . . .

Our pictures of the join-up were radioed around the world. The BBC announced that the first men to get through 'had made history', so when it was unkindly suggested we had only returned to relish a night or two in the Naples Officers' Club, we were able to reply with nonchalant modesty, 'Just made history, old boy – that's all . . .'

After a couple of days of baths, booze and broads, as they say, it was eerie returning from Naples past Monte Cassino and through the old German lines to the poor battered Anzio seafront villa that had protected us for so long. We now needed to position ourselves to cover the imminent breakout north towards Rome.

We found that with an open road from the base areas almost to the front line, the Anzio Bridgehead was disappearing and taking with it the Anzio spirit. This had been tangible and heartening – and understandable because so many thousands of us had been together and desperate, for so long.

Unlike any other war-front I have covered, there was total equality of sacrifice: we were all on the chopping block, all within range. You could never get out of the war, even for a moment. Shells and bombs are great levellers – if they don't kill you, they bring you together. For once Generals were in almost as much danger as Corporals. Anzio was a place apart from the rest of the struggling world.

I detected, however, that the beleaguered men of the Beachhead regarded the relieving troops with slight resentment – not as rescuers, but as trespassers, intruders. Like its predecessor, Tobruk, Anzio had become the most exclusive club in the world – membership restricted to those who for months had endured the fighting, the ceaseless bombing and shelling, the dying. We had grown close. Even the GIs were all right – often *better* than all right.

But now the perimeter was dissolving. Strange tidy men with different battledress-flashes and clean boots appeared, driving vehicles with another shade of camouflage, looking at maps and longing for Rome. There were even a few spotless staff cars with Base Wallahs from Naples and Caserta, smart amid our filthy encrusted jeeps.

The bridgehead we had defended for so long was being taken over – by *our* side . . .

HITLER WOULD HAVE HAD HIM SHOT . . .

Though victory was in the air, other battlefields awaited, just ahead. Before dawn on June 3 '44 I was driving through front lines now deserted, out from Anzio and along the Appian Way, past slow-moving columns of tanks and troop carriers. I was on my way to liberate Rome! There was a Bank Holiday atmosphere until, five miles from the city boundary, we were stopped by shellfire – just as we had been 17 weeks before. A bloody-minded German 88mm was making a last stand around the corner. We waited impatiently for our tanks to deal with it. This was no time to join the ranks of stretcher cases.

A commotion down the road behind us – and then a dozen Italians in their Sunday best came strolling and chattering along, heading happily towards the German position. It was a spring-time wedding party – the bride too determined to get to the church on time to bother with a mere war.

They waved their flowers at us, sedate and smiling. We shouted warnings, but they had other matters on their minds and strolled on in a jolly procession around the corner towards the church – and the 88mm. We waited, fearful, for one shell to ring out. Silence.

An hour later they returned, well churched. We drew breath again. Everything had evidently been signed and sealed, to general satisfaction. The German gunners had been understanding, and we too gave the happy couple an enthusiastic round of applause as they strolled away to their reception. We, however, were still pinned down. Every movement towards the city brought another shell, so we had growing admiration for that former signorina with an acute sense of priorities who proved you *can* get a man with a gun – or despite a gun – even if it is the enemy's.

We could not all get married but we *could* all get shot so, growing cautious at this stage of the war, we gave the gun best and retreated to Anzio for another night.

By first light next morning the 88mm had gone and we drove carefully around that corner into an apparently peaceful Rome. On our way through empty shopping streets we suddenly emerged in front of the symbol of the eternity of the city: the Colosseum, grandest and most celebrated of all its monuments. An ancient belief warns that if the Colosseum falls, Rome will fall – and the whole world will follow. Indeed, that is what happened to the Axis.

This falling, on a sunny June morning, was gentle. In the amphitheatre, no Christians were being thrown to the lions, so far, and for the first time for four months no Allied or German gladiators were fighting to the death along the roads to Rome. All was peaceful.

As we arrived the Piazzale del Colosseo was deserted but for a couple of hesitant motor scooters wondering where to go to celebrate. At the 'wedding cake', the overbearing marble monument to Victor Emmanuel II completed in 1911 upon the unification of Italy, two armed guards stood traditionally to attention at the tomb of the Unknown Soldier. Usually an unnoticed feature in that white monumental landscape, they were now in the best position to view a happy and noisy kaleidoscope of a day. As I went up to salute they half-smiled politely into the distance, gladiators no longer.

Back in 1922, at the start of it all, the Duce reached this spot, weary after the 'March on Rome'. He presented himself to the King, apologising for his bowler hat and spats and saying, improbably: 'I come from the battlefield.' In fact he came from the overnight express from Milan at 10.30am, but the 'March' was a required myth of Fascism, as were the fictitious 3,000 martyrs who supposedly died in the insurrection which had brought Mussolini to the capital.

Another 3,000 Blackshirts were also missing the day, 23 years later, when other Italians came to murder Mussolini.

Just across the piazza a small crowd was gathering outside the Palazzo Venezia, the 15th century palace which was Mussolini's official residence. I pushed through these early celebrants and climbed the marble stairs to take a look at the Duce's second-floor salon. Its dimensions were suitably Dictatorial – two storeys high, 70 feet long by 40 feet wide, and well-designed to show Adolf Hitler how Leaders *ought* to live. From the door to the Duce's desk in that vast empty chamber you had to cover 60-feet of marble and mosaic – quite a long march, if you were in trouble.

I slipped outside to stand briefly on the small shallow balcony overlooking the piazza from where Mussolini harangued his empire, and the world. I modestly pretended not to hear the cries of 'Speech!' from a growing crowd. I just haven't got the gestures . . .

This day was proving a tranquil and so far enjoyable inter-mission, after a particularly nasty phase in our war. Perhaps now we should not need to fight for Rome, street by street? Unbearable to think of the Colosseum as another Cassino . . .

Fortunately it seemed that Hitler had appreciated the worldwide distress which followed our bombing of Cassino Monastery, and was aware that any destruction within the Eternal City would be internationally condemned. At this stage of the war Rome could not be defended, so had little strategic or tactical value. On June 2 Kesselring requested Hitler's permission to evacuate the city without fighting. At the same time Pope Pius XII warned, 'Whoever raises a hand against Rome will be guilty of matricide to the whole civilised world and in the eternal judgment of God.' To general relief Hitler then issued a Führer Decision: the capital must not become a battlefield. It would not be defended, even if attacked.

However there was little tolerance on the Allied side, for Rome had been the focal point of German lines of supply. Reinforcements and military supplies passed through the capital day and night, by rail and road, to the Anzio and Cassino fronts. 'Open City' was an empty propaganda phrase.

Earlier a Churchill telegram to President Roosevelt had explained: 'We think it would be a mistake to talk about making Rome an Open City as it may hamper our forward movement and will anyway not bind the enemy.' In the House of Commons the Foreign Secretary Anthony Eden was not conciliatory: 'Britain has as much right to bomb Rome as the Italians had to bomb London.'

Strangely enough it was Mussolini who was said to have requested that his capital be defended street-by-street, to the horror of Romans. Was he *really* calling for another Stalingrad? In Rome it was believed that public services, bridges and main hotels had already been mined by the Germans. Now passersby silently observed another army in retreat from their capital, as officers' luggage was driven away from Via Veneto hotels.

On June 3 the last of the Wehrmacht engineers waiting to blow up the Eternal City packed their detonators and began a peaceful withdrawal across the undamaged bridges over the Tiber. They were heading for the Gothic Line 180 miles to the north where, across the Arno, there were other beautiful and ancient bridges to destroy.

Without hearing a single explosion, we set about getting our long-delayed liberation pictures. After drab demolished Anzio we marvelled at the peacetime cleanliness of Rome, the excitement and joy at its restored freedom and safety, the absence of war damage, the bright and elegant women, the welcome . . . In that vibrant capital it was hard to believe the daily bread ration had been 100 grams a day – two slices. The Holy See was providing the starving poor with 100,000 meals a day, and water-sellers were on the streets.

We did not then know that our Commanding General had deliberately allowed the German armies to escape the crushing defeat planned for them, that his fixation about liberating Rome had turned into an obsession, and that mainly because of him Allied troops – including the US forces – would be fighting and dying in Italy for another year.

After breaking-out of Anzio, Alexander's plan – *Diadem* – devised by his Chief of Staff Lieutenant General Sir John Harding, was for the Fifth Army to drive north and east out of Anzio to cut Kesselring's escape route, trapping and then destroying his Tenth and Fourteenth Armies. The liberation of Rome was a secondary objective.

The operation started well, though Churchill disguised his concern in a telegram to Field Marshal Alexander: 'The glory of this battle, already great, will be measured not by the capture of Rome or the juncture with the bridgehead, but by the number of German divisions cut off . . . It is the cop that counts.'

Not to General Mark Clark, who then seemed quite indifferent to the fate of those enemy divisions. Churchill was unaware of the manoeuvre Clark had already put into action, overriding *Diadem*. When our leading troops were four miles away from closing the trap at Valmontone on Highway 6 and so controlling all road and rail lines between Cassino and Rome, the US VI Corps was suddenly redirected north towards Rome. The trap was left open. This was General Clark's hidden plan to ensure that he alone would capture Rome, and the headlines.

He had not been shy about his determination to be the sole Liberator of the first Axis capital to fall. Earlier Alexander had reminded him of the perceptive Churchill's concern that the massive non-American role in the capture of Rome by at least six other nations might be publicly ignored. In addition to our Eighth Army, the British had as many divisions in the Fifth Army as did Americans. There were also Poles, Indians, New Zealanders, South Africans and French.

Clark's reaction to a sharing of the headlines and public relations spoils, was fury. He told the Field Marshal that if he gave him such an order he would refuse to obey, and if Eighth Army men tried to advance upon Rome he would order his Fifth Army troops to fire on them.

That must surely be the first time a threat of bloody and violent mutiny against his own side has ever been uttered by an Allied General to his Commander. Alexander, who rarely asserted himself in such cases, chose not to hear that mutinous outburst.

The distinguished American military historian Carlo d'Este wrote, 'Clark's calculated act was to prove as militarily stupid as it was insubordinate. He deliberately committed what must rank as one of the most misguided blunders made by any Allied Commander during World War II. About to win a stunning victory that would not only have given him the flattering prize of Rome virtually without a fight, but would have earned him immortality as a great battlefield Commander, Mark Clark suddenly dismembered Operation *Buffalo*.' (Alexander's plan to cut Highway 6 at Valmontone).

With his Fifth Army about to entrap Kesselring's exhausted Tenth and Fourteenth Armies, General Clark redirected it north towards Rome, turning his triumphant army away from a broken enemy. He left a token force in a half-hearted attempt to contain the retreating Germans, but allowing a delighted Kesselring to lead his escaping armies north while the Hermann Goering Division reached Valmontone and held the escape route open. With Mark Clark on his side, Kesselring easily extricated his two armies from the now enfeebled trap.

General Clark had already made sure that the British divisions serving under him were safely out of the way, pursuing the enemy along the *high* road, the mountainous route through central Italy. His US units took the *low* road, towards Rome.

He also took care to leave his radio and telephone off the hook, so he would not be available to answer any of the outraged calls by incredulous and angry subordinates. He withheld all Fifth Army information from Field Marshal Alexander for 24 hours, until it was too late for his orders to be reversed. General Truscott was dumbfounded and demanded to talk to Clark, who of course was 'not available and out of radio contact'. So, like a good soldier, Truscott swallowed hard and loyally carried-out the unusual order to throw away a victory.

Clark's self-created Race for Rome had been so outrageous that he forfeited the respect of Truscott and earned the outright contempt of Brigadier General Robert Frederick, Commander of the US Special Forces, who complained that he had been compelled to lose men so that Clark could enter Rome while the light was right for pictures. Major General Francis Tuker, the clever Commander of the 4th Indian Division in the Fifth Army at Cassino described him as 'a flashy ignoramus'.

So Mark Clark, totally absorbed with self-publicity, remained the Germans' favourite enemy General: he always gave them an easier time than they expected – and with his strong personality, always got away with it.

Back in Washington the 36th Division Veterans' Association had demanded that the US Congress investigate Clark's handling of the disastrous Rapido offensive that had crippled their division after a hopeless attack which cost 1,681 men without even disturbing the Germans. Clark was finally exonerated, though his amateurish operation would not have been necessary had he been willing to exploit the success four days earlier of Lieutenant General McCreery, his X Corps Commander. But then Richard McCreery, who despised Clark, was British. Better no victory, Clark must have reasoned, than a shared victory.

I watched General Clark arrive in St Peter's Square that morning, not knowing he had neutralised all foreign and competitive divisions under his command. He was sitting in the front of an open jeep, its screen flat, his Chief of Staff Major General Gruenther perched behind him. The light was good for pictures. He was followed, not by his Fifth Army, but by his regular phalanx of War Correspondents.

The first thing he did was to hold a Press conference along the balustrade of the City Hall, posing for pictures against ancient Roman buildings and pretending he had been discussing the battle situation with his Commanders before being 'surprised' by his escorting Press.

An experienced correspondent friend of mine from London, the much-respected Eric Sevareid of CBS, was one of those offended by Clark's insensitive claims for glory and failure to mention in his victory proclamation the British, French, Poles, New Zealanders and South Africans who had also fought to liberate Rome. Sevareid wrote, 'It was not apparently a great day for the world, for the Allies, for all the suffering people who had desperately looked toward the time of peace. It was a great day for the Fifth Army. The men of the Eighth Army whose sector did not happen to include Rome but without whose efforts this day could not have occurred, did not soon forget the remark.

'Clark spread a map on the balustrade and proceeded to point out something or other to his Commanders. The cameras ground, the Corps Commanders – red with embarrassment – looked back and forth from us to the map. A colleague commented, "On this historic occasion, I feel like vomiting."'

General Clark personally reviewed important Press and radio despatches before transmission from his headquarters, so censored much of Sevareid's despatch.

Clark's vainglorious blunder, the worst of the entire War in my experience, lost us a stunning victory, lengthened the war by many months, cost numberless lives and earned Mark Clark the amazed contempt of other American and British Generals. They saw an operation that could have won the war in Italy thrown away at a fearful price in lives because of the vanity of one man. If General Mark Clark had been in the German army, Adolf Hitler would have had him shot.

As it was the US nurtured him, though he spent the remainder of a long life attempting to justify his decision before Rome, and doctoring his war diaries. It may have prevented him becoming President, but there are always honorific positions for a former Army Commander. The ultimate survivor, he went on to take over the Fifteenth Army Group as a four-star General in place of Field Marshal Alexander, who became Supreme Commander. He was appointed US High Commissioner in Austria, and C-in-C

of the United Nations Command at the Peace talks in Korea . . .
His brother-officers observed the Rise and Rise of Markus
Clarkus with considerable scorn.

While General Clark was relishing his triumphant entry, most
of the men of his Army were already pushing north in an unsuccessful attempt to catch Kesselring's escaping rearguard before
it reached the security of their Gothic Line across Italy.

However two days after the liberation of Rome, the victory
pictures and newspaper stories he longed for were as dust, and
ignored. It was another D-Day – the big one. The long-awaited
Allied invasion of Normandy had begun. The Second Front took
over the headlines and the liberation of Rome became yester-
day's news, relegated to inside pages. We had won an Axis capital
– but lost our audience.

General Mark Clark was a striking and attractive man with
bony face and beak nose. He looked like a Red Indian chief.
Churchill had called him, admiringly, 'The American Eagle' –
until he tumbled him. His vanity was remarkable – he could have
given lessons to any Hollywood prima donna. Even during the
desperate days of the war when we were hard-pressed to hold
our ground he kept a publicity machine of some 50 men around
him and insisted his permanent cameraman only took pictures
from the left – his best side, he believed.

Every state-of-the-war communication from his Headquarters
had to have 'Lieutenant General Mark W. Clark's Fifth Army'
three times on the first page and once every page thereafter
– yes, this *is* the Army, Mrs Jones. His publicity machine even
produced a Fifth Army song beginning, 'Stand up stand up for
General Clark, let's sing the praises of General Clark . . .' During
an early performance at Allied headquarters, Caserta, the General stood stiffly to attention during this evangelical adoration.
It was not like Sandhurst at all . . .

In fact less than a third of the troops in General Mark W. Clark's international Fifth Army were American, yet we had to get used to American ways.

I know from my own experience that during the height of the war when it seemed we might be losing, an American despatch rider drew up at my campsite with an urgent service message from the Commanding General. I opened it anxiously, expecting dramatic orders.

The signal began: 'Captain Whicker, my calendar tells me that today is your birthday. May I . . .' etc etc. It was a Greetings Telegram from the Commanding General, thrown up by his filing system and delivered amid shot and shell to a ditch near the front line, while most of us were busy trying to win the war! I showed this unusual communication to an American friend, Captain John Ford, who sniffed and said, 'He's running for President.'

There's a postscript: thirty-two years later I was filming a *Whicker's World* for Yorkshire TV in Charleston, South Carolina, and took my cameras to the Citadel, the US military college with their Army's strictest discipline. General Clark, now retired from the Army, was seeing his Service out as its President. He was living with a scornful and unsympathetic second wife in the college President's House – though would surely have much preferred the White House. She was the widow of an army colleague, and not given to hero-worship: 'If he catches a cold,' she told me 'Walter Reed Hospital spends half a million dollars trying to cure him.' Over 80 and still convinced he had done nothing wrong at Rome, the total self-belief, good looks and charm remained.

After our talk he swept my lady Valerie out into his garden, cut her a rose and presented it with a flourish. *She* would have voted for him.

It is curious that by chance I should have taken the pictures for which Mark Clark changed the course of the War. I had got into the heart of Rome in my solitary jeep some time before he arrived and was taking pictures outside St Peter's when his jeep burst through streets crowded with anxious Romans, followed by his motorcade of Correspondents and cameramen.

I moved away to the Capitol, and once again happened to be at the top of a monumental staircase when he arrived with some of his Generals. My pictures of him leading them up the steps went around the world – indeed, I saw one had pride of place in his home, commemorating his finest hour.

Italian partisans were also emerging to beat-up Fascists or settle old grudges. A few stern girl communists were parading home-made red flags. The cafés were crowded, preparing for the start of *La Dolce Vita*. On the Via Veneto *bella figura* had begun its takeover – already the Italians were far more elegant than their weary liberators, though dusty GIs were applauded. The first British arrived – some had fought 2,500 miles from Egypt and were still looking for a good cup of tea. The first barbershops were lifting their shutters; we dived into one for the full treatment. As Peter Hopkinson said, 'You don't shave yourself when you've just liberated Rome.'

Pope Pius XII was also alert to the bad international press he had received for not reacting strongly against Hitler's concentration camps and anti-Semitism. He received Correspondents in audience at the Vatican, blessed us and thanked both parties for sparing the City. There was a flurry among small gum-chewing New York photographers who all seemed to be called Bernie Goldstein. With great half-plate cameras and determined ambulance-chasing approach, they were a breath of peacetime push and noticeably unawed by the grandeur of the Vatican. It restored equilibrium to hear those urgent cries in Brooklynese: 'Hold it, Pope!'

That evening, having held it many times, His Holiness appeared on the balcony before a crowd of 200,000 Italians, most of them weeping with joy and emotion. The Pope thanked God and the warring nations for sparing Rome and as he raised his hands in benediction, I had planned to remain standing and take that great dramatic picture over their bowed heads.

The multitude around me sank to its knees for the blessing. I attempted to remain on my feet – but could not. Against my will I was drawn down with them, camera dangling ineffectually at my chest. I remained there during the blessing. It was the end of the capital's first day of freedom.

The Roman spring of '44 was a heady blend of elegance, romance and sensory overkill. The horror that was Anzio now meant that even normality was exciting, and each new pleasure intensified beyond belief. Every day was perfect: the sun shone, the food was rich and different, the wines new and seductive, the hotel sheets crisp and scented, the comfortable baths old and deep, the girls enchanting, the sweet life of the Via Veneto already brilliant, everyone smiled – and we were winning!

Public Relations took over the Hotel de la Ville in the Via Sistina above the incomparable Spanish Steps up which, returning from various celebrations in the small hours, I would on occasion drive my jeep, starting at the Piazza d'Espagna. It was a bumpy but triumphant ride, requiring a certain delicacy, but seemed a more effective victory gesture than merely stealing a policeman's helmet on New Year's Eve in Piccadilly Circus; and we knew we would never ever be able to do anything as wicked again, after the war.

So we found ourselves living in comfort within the heart of the Eternal City, and life became just as perfect as could be. It was like peacetime, only better.

A BEAUTIFUL WOMAN WITH HER TEETH
KNOCKED OUT . . .

The German armies, having avoided capture, were falling back according to plan on their Gothic Line along mountains running 125 miles across Italy, north of Florence, to wait for the winter. They delayed our pursuit where they could: blown bridges, landmines, air raids, demolitions, local counter-attacks . . .

For those unleashed from the claustrophobic bridgehead it was exciting enough just to drive after them along open roads through glorious countryside, past Lake Bolsena and the cathedral at Orvieto, through Perugia and Assisi and the three hills of Siena.

Like schoolboys at end-of-term we were relaxed and free and sped through timeless Tuscan landscapes, already triumphant. The world had suddenly become wide, the horizon distant, the future seductive.

I had left liberated Rome reluctantly, but dutifully, to pursue the armies. Anticlimactic it felt, probably wrongly – but at least no one was shooting at us, so far. Once in Florence I softened the blow by requisitioning for our headquarters a delightful villa just out of town, on a hillock overlooking the Arno Valley with views towards Fiesole – at least this one was rat-free and not shelled every day. Called Villa Paradisino and well named, it belonged to a pleasant Italian ship-owner, Ludovico Daneo with his vivacious Russian wife Patsya and young son of my age, Francescino. We became friends for life.

Florence has always seemed to me the ideal city in which to live. Few places on earth have been so civilised for so long, spared what we now call Progress, and most wars – except ours, when thankfully most major destruction was avoided. Within its classic Tuscan countryside it had a sort of elegant enchantment that seemed planned down to the last cypress. Like Venice, it was the perfect size for stylish city life. There was always time and space for friends and, should you glimpse a pretty girl shopping in the Via Tornabuoni she would not disappear for ever, but within a day or two would surely materialise again, tantalisingly within reach and distantly related to your neighbour who had invited her for drinks next Sunday.

We had missed our pictures at the Gestapo headquarters in Rome – 155 Via Tasso – so as we approached Florence I put two cameramen with a special Commando unit that was to capture the SS Headquarters at Villa Spellman, and its monsters. They found it locked and empty.

The Eighth Army had been elbowed out of the Liberation of Rome, but at least Winston Churchill flew to the Mediterranean to salute us . . . He watched the Royal Artillery firing at new German positions and on one shell chalked, 'To Hitler, from Churchill'. To his great satisfaction, it was then fired at the enemy.

'It's like writing a rude letter' he said, 'and being there when it arrives!'

German army engineers who since Sicily had blown almost every bridge, flyover, aqueduct and tunnel they saw – except those over the Tiber – compensated for that solitary gesture by destroying all the graceful bridges across the Arno except the incomparable Ponte Vecchio, where they blew up its surroundings. Florence looked like a beautiful woman with her teeth knocked out.

We never found an answer to the Germans' horrifyingly efficient tactics which achieved massive destruction, but only short delays. In an attempt to limit further damage, the Eighth Army kept a loose hold on the city up to the banks of the Arno, leaving the partisans to deal with remaining enemy on the northern side. With little idea of street fighting, they conducted a vigorous but unscientific war. I watched one group attempting to throw grenades across the wide Arno. It had become a war game – amateurs versus professionals – which they fought with spirit, but scores were killed or wounded by German snipers, who were not playing.

Two of my Sergeants were taking pictures in a central hospital overflowing with such casualties, while their driver chatted to a weary young Italian doctor and some nurses. In stumbling but well-meant army-Italian, with gestures, Driver Wood attempted to confide that he came from Sheffield, the city where they made the steel for their surgical instruments.

This news was received with unexpected enthusiasm. He then found himself escorted around the wards and asked incomprehensible questions. He shook his head when it seemed suitable, or nodded approvingly. They reached an operating theatre where a partisan with his chest blown open lay upon the table. The young doctor asked Driver Wood for help with the operation.

A nice obliging lad, Wood was willing to turn his hand to anything. Fortunately I arrived at that moment and snatched the scalpel away as he approached the unconscious man in a businesslike manner, as though tackling a stalled jeep . . .

*　*　*

The last Germans had withdrawn, or surrendered, when the first of our Army patrols came clambering over the ruins around both ends of the 1345 Ponte Vecchio with its tiny 16th century shops. They found the heart of the city undamaged. The weary infantry-men trudged through the glory that is Florence, where each palace looks like a fortress. They passed the most famous statue in the world, Michelangelo's David – and the 1296 cathedral complex of the Duomo – without a second glance. The symbols of Tuscan pride have limited impact when you've walked here from Sicily . . .

The Allied armies now faced a more serious slog through the Gothic Line, the final and elaborate defensive position run-ning across Italy, constructed by German engineers through the Apennines from the Tyrrhenian Sea to Pesaro on the Adriatic. As the Wehrmacht was slowly beaten-back, Italy had provided some of the hardest fighting of World War II – and this was perhaps the most formidable of her natural obstacles.

When winter closed-in and the rains and snow came, our push north ground to a halt. There was some local fighting, for it was certainly not all over yet. On the Eighth Army's Adriatic front the Canadians captured Rimini, then Ravenna. Mussolini had been demanding some action from his Republican divisions in the German armies, so on Christmas Eve the Germans, sen-sing weakness and preoccupation with the Holiday, ordered a sudden counter-attack by the German-equipped Italian Monte Rosa Division down the east coast towards Lucca. It was the Italians' first warlike gesture, and they were attended by 16 Panzer Grenadiers.

This tiny token presence seemed to be effective, for the Italians routed the US 92nd Negro Division and its supporting Brazilian expeditionary force. They all fled, allowing the Monte Rosas to capture Barga and occupy both banks of the River Serchio just north of Lucca, which threatened the Fifth Army's communications with the port of Livorno.

That unexpected enemy victory had an equally unexpected effect in Florence, where stylish social life was resuming. Cautious society mothers heard of this Allied defeat and, moving fast, would not allow their daughters to attend any more Savoy Hotel tea dances in case German and Fascist officers should return victorious and expectant, and recapture the ballroom floor. This would demand a quick-quick change of partners.

On the warfront, the Fifth Army borrowed the 8th Indian Division from the Eighth Army to rectify the embarrassing rout. It quickly re-established both the territory of the departed 92nd Division *and* the tea dances, thus allowing the Generals of the resting armies to build-up strength for the final battles to come in springtime, and the sensitive Florentine mothers to rearrange peacefully their dance lists of marriageable daughters and promising partners.

As at Anzio, winter fighting in the Gothic Line had become trench warfare. Food and ammo had to be carried up to mountain positions by mules. When they gave up, men carried on. Our pictures showed grim shell-shattered front-line villages in the mud and snow looking horribly like the Somme or Passchendaele, where in icy numbing wretchedness the PBI had to survive conditions their Great War fathers knew only too well.

Kesselring's delaying tactics had again postponed defeat and won another extension of a war which should have ended after Anzio, before his retreating armies could reach the sanctuary of the Gothic Line. There as planned they could easily hold up the weary Allies until the Apennine winter came to the Germans' rescue and the mountainous war-front froze.

Front-line life during the stalemate became as still as Anzio had been furious. Nobody was winning or losing – indeed there was little fighting. Surviving was difficult enough. Each day I would visit my teams in their mountain positions north of the Futa Pass or at various headquarters – divisional, battalion, company – and in the evening race down through the mountains back to Florence and Paradisino; only 30 miles, but the contrast was cruel.

With cameramen scattered around the Army, we could rarely all get together, so would usually find ourselves at some other unit's celebration on high days and holidays; but AFPU quickly developed character and a strong flavour, always curious, always poking its lens into other people's lives, always welcomed as a direct link to home. I still have pictures of our memorable Christmas party at the villa showing us having as jolly a time as is possible, without girls.

My two Lieutenants would be out in the field with our camera teams, or would return from the Front for a wash-and-brush-up at Paradisino and a night in *Fascisissimo Firenze,* as Mussolini called it.

I remember Lieutenant George Groom coming in triumphantly with a splendid pair of suede desert boots he had somehow obtained from Cairo. He was planning to wear them on important occasions to show he had been a Desert Rat.

Hughes, my young Welsh batman, took a lot of time and trouble polishing them into a distinctive hairy shine. This was not appreciated, and when the shouting died down George returned sourly to Officers' Shop brown boots.

After the winter months of skirmishing, the Fifth and Eighth Armies awaited the spring to launch the final attacks that would win the war. On the north side of the Futa Pass we broke through to capture Bologna on April 19, and a week later I was able to cross the Po on the heels of the retreating Fourteenth Army and reach Verona, provincial capital adopted by Shakespeare for Romeo and Juliet. Look – that's their balcony!

Everywhere the Germans were falling back towards the Alps and defeat; not with relief, but with anger. You would have to be *very* unlucky indeed to be killed or wounded at this stage of the war but, as in the ruins of Cassino, many suicidal last-ditch paratroops and fanatical SS still wanted to take us with them. Mines and booby traps also knew nothing of armistice negotiations or peace moves, and partisans with stolen guns were always a little uncertain whom they should shoot next, in a good cause. On April 25 there was a general uprising and in some towns partisans seized control.

Trying to cover our disintegrating war I found myself among the pursuers and by then, pursuing in some style as befitted a victor in a large and unmilitary coach-built Fiat Coupé liberated from the partisans who'd captured it from the Germans who'd stolen it. We all found it so much cosier than those chilly jeeps.

I had spent much of the war in jeeps – a marvellous vehicle in almost every way except that it was not comfortable and had little or no weather protection. In winter it was cold and wet as it bounced around – like driving a lifeboat through a stormy sea. So in my army career the object of the exercise was usually to try and capture some wheels that were just a bit cosy.

That Opel Kapitan convertible the King admired had been perfect for a Tunisian summer, but the snow-covered Apennines in winter and even the rainswept Po Valley in early spring called for something with windows and heater.

Even today, after more than 60 years, that Fiat Coupé still strikes me as a good-looking car. Then it was Ultimate Luxury: it carried me towards the end of the war – and eventually, out of it – in enviable style.

To the east the Eighth had also fought through the Gothic Line and into the Po Valley. I was still supposedly with the Fifth, but after all our fast movement and their indecision, seemed to have mislaid it somewhere. Feeling lonely after the hurly-burly, I drove on into Verona and took over as AFPU billet the stately villa of the *Sicherheitspolizei*, Germany's State Secret Police. It was empty but very clean, and to my surprise had none of the bad vibes of former Gestapo buildings still oppressed by terror and silent screams.

Now I just hoped that all the vengeful and heavily-armed partisans aimlessly wandering the city looking for someone to shoot . . . were aware there had been a change of tenant.

The radio announced that the German forces in Northern Italy had been cut in two. The capture and liberation of Verona by Allied troops was also expected soon. This was disconcerting because I had been living there for several days. They might have told me.

OUT-GUNNED ON ONE SIDE, OUT-SCREAMED ON THE OTHER . . .

One morning, impatient with our Army for not catching up and hoping the war was over, I set out from the quiet and ancient city and headed through the Po Valley into enemy territory. I needed to find out what was happening to the climax of our battles, one way or the other.

I struck directly west along the autostrada towards the industrial complex of Milan, economic capital of Italy which had been bombed 15 times. The splendid road avoided Brescia and Bergamo, and the flat countryside seemed empty and suspect. I had not seen an army – ours or theirs – for several days. It seemed the enemy had gone – and *we* hadn't arrived. . . Yet somewhere within this silent landscape, a war was ending.

Most of the Eighth must have turned right after capturing Padua and Venice, and headed for Venezia Giulia; in Trieste and Istria they still had Tito to handle. The Fifth had probably dispersed towards Turin. After Rome and Mark Clark's climax, it seemed to have lost its sense of direction – or perhaps it was me?

With a few diversions for blown bridges I reached Milan without even seeing a German or being shot-at. This was already an improvement. I drove on cautiously through the shuttered streets of the vast city into its very heart: the Piazza del Duomo, Cathedral Square, and its magnificent Gothic monument with 135 spires which the Milanese began building in 1386 and completed in 1813. Italians have always been relaxed about work schedules.

Now the place was empty and silent. I seemed to have captured Milan, without anyone noticing. Like one of those ominous End-of-the-World films, I was the last man alive.

As I was taking my first shots, the calm was abruptly shattered when a bunch of apocalyptic partisans tumbled into the piazza, shouting, and raced up to me. I was no longer the last man alive.

It seemed they had surrounded the headquarters of Hitler's SS in a nearby hotel but the heavily armed storm troopers occupying it were still resisting and would only surrender to an Allied officer. So far, they said, I was the only one in town.

I knew about the SS – they were the special police force founded by Hitler as his personal bodyguard back in 1925, at the start of it all. As the Nazi machine grew in size they began to provide Germany's security forces – including the Gestapo – and administered its concentration camps. Despite those nightmare roles the *Schutzstaffel* (defence squadron) regarded itself as an elite. The SS were feared and loathed, even within the German armed forces; tough and skilled, they believed they made the Law.

I had been looking for pictures, not prisoners – and especially not SS prisoners – but allowed the frenzied group to bustle me along the Via Manzoni towards La Scala, most famous opera house in the world.

In the distance I could *hear* where their trouble was: an Italian crowd, growing hysterical and working-up its bloodlust. The whole central area was rapidly changing from deserted to crammed. Any Milanese brave enough to face the uncertainty of the streets was converging upon this last outpost, to be in at the kill.

Half way along, a large corner building on the right was ringed by layers of high barbed wire barriers on wooden frames. These held back a growing mass of jeering Italians. Behind the wire stood scores of sullen SS men with machine guns, a finger on every trigger. Bigger guns were sticking out of most upstairs windows.

The silent disciplined troopers, facing a lynching, regarded me impassively. Until this morning they had been running the show; people stepped off the pavement before them. Now they were preparing to go down fighting in a suicidal last stand, taking with them as many Milanese as could be shot in the time available. Facing them through the barbed wire, the crush of noisy Italians was giving voice to its opinion of the German army, with gestures. This was going to be the final action of the SS in Italy, the last hurrah. It was not, I felt, a suitable moment to join the trend, and get shot.

However, leaving my partisans amid their crowd, pushing aside my sense of survival and accepting an uncertain future as a possible SS hostage, I strode past the German guard posts and into the hotel. Inside the barricades an impeccable SS General in a black uniform was waiting in the lobby. He clicked his heels, saluted and handed me his revolver. I could sense he was politely concealing disappointment at my lowly rank. 'My men are at your disposal,' he said, in English. 'We could not surrender to that . . . *rabble.*' Scornful gesture at the surrounding clamour.

I could understand his reluctance. Once disarmed his men would surely have been shot – or more likely, torn to pieces. In this furious stand-off there was now nothing between the hated SS and the partisans . . . except me, with my puny .38 Smith and

Wesson – now reinforced by the General's more effective Walther. I could take over and attempt to deal with the tumult of jeers and threats facing the menace of SS automatic weapons . . . or walk away and ignore a devastating eruption of rage and revenge – a final bloody massacre in the streets.

It was evident I was out-gunned on one side, out-screamed on the other. All I had in support was the limited authority of three pips, a British battledress and a growing but foolhardy determination not to be pushed around by the heel-clicking remnants of an army we had just beaten in a fair fight, or by a jeering mob.

Acting the stern victor, I told the General that the local uproar must be ignored, that any shooting by his men would now be a war crime and duly punished, that American armour would soon be arriving when the Italian crowds would be dispersed and he and his men escorted into captivity. I had no idea of course that all this would actually *happen*, but with so many guns waving about on both sides of the wire it seemed wise to reassure everyone about everything.

There's never a friendly armoured division around when you need one.

Much fury and hatred seethed in that street, for in the last year some very bad things had been done in Italy by the Germans – mainly by the SS and the Gestapo: the massacre of 335 Roman hostages in the Ardeatine Caves was a recent horror.

I decided it would be wise to go outside the hotel occasionally and display myself, passing through the barbed wire so the hostile mob could see some progress: one Allied officer at least was taking an interest. I repeated this authoritative performance a few times during the afternoon, hoping it might relieve the pressure and prevent some enraged hothead deciding that an Italian mob in good voice could take-on a building full of SS machine guns, if it was angry enough. They kept shouting and I kept moving and the SS kept watching. The balance seemed to work.

Looking back from the relative security and sanity of today, it seems too much to hope that a lone and youthful Captain would even consider trying to control a frenzied Italian mob *and* a desperate but highly professional unit of German SS – yet war and rank bring instant maturity and authority. In the army, orders are obeyed; it is quite unthinkable that they would *not* be obeyed. All I had planned to do was to take a few relaxed pictures of the Cathedral, but now I was presiding over the last stand of Hitler's killers.

These things happen.

As though I did not have enough to worry about, at that moment the SS Adjutant came downstairs followed by two of his men struggling with a heavy tin trunk which they handled as though full of dynamite. I allowed myself to be drawn into a corner of the lobby to watch him open it – and then understood why they were so tense.

It must have been the Treasury of the SS in Italy, for it was crammed to the brim with every type of currency, in precise Germanic order. Piles of familiar lire, sterling and dollars of course, with pesetas and kronor, flamboyant Swiss francs and reichsmarks, and a lot of crisp exotic notes I did not recognise. I had never seen so much varied currency in one place – and never have since.

Having ensured that I understood our transaction, the precise Adjutant locked and secured those many millions, handed me the key with a half-smile, saluted and withdrew – his war was over. Mine was not.

It occurred to me in a happy flash that what I *ought* to do was to accept my remarkable luck and order them to place Aladdin's trunk in my unmarked car for safekeeping. It was a legitimate spoil of war, surrendered to me by the enemy. Then at a suitable moment during the day's chaotic climax I would make my excuses and drive south, back through our lines to the Villa Paradisino where my Florentine friends would look after it for a year or two, no questions asked. When the wartime dust had settled I would return and, like Ali Baba, open it – and set about becoming very rich indeed. Shouldn't be too difficult. If I did not accept the trophy, someone else certainly would. It seemed like a good idea, at the time.

After several hours of noisy confusion during which I held the growing mob at bay and untruthfully reassured an increasingly nervous SS Command that I had their surrender well under control, an American tank regiment *did* arrive to liberate Milan, to my surprise and delight. I was the only one who had *not* believed my story!

In the late afternoon, attracted by the uproar in our street, Shermans of the good old US 1st Armoured Division clattered up to the hotel (as I had promised) and were well received by one and all. At the sight of armour and troops, the crowd calmed down and the SS began hesitantly to pile their machine guns in the hotel lobby.

Then, having made a life-changing decision, I handed my priceless trunk over to the American Colonel, along with my German General and all my SS men. They were about to be prisoners, while I was about to be . . . demobbed and looking for a job. It was all written in the stars.

So, give or take a couple of dozen cruel murders, that was almost the end of Whicker's War – and on quite a high note, too. From then on it was downhill all the way, financially.

Never again in a crowded life was I to be offered a trunkful of money...

The city's mood had changed by the time my SS men drove themselves away in buses and trucks towards a prison camp, under the protective guns of the tanks. My iron discipline had been removed – or perhaps it was their automatics – but as they passed through streets now jammed solid, the jeering crowd hit out at any open car they could reach with fists and attaché cases and umbrellas – though no weapons that could kill. Some storm troopers in the moving vehicles tried to fight back at such an indignity – but their fighting days were over and they must have been thankful to be getting out alive.

My Aladdin's trunk disappeared forever into the Allied war machine, and I returned to taking the pictures I had neglected during my brief but pivotal role amid the ruins of Hitler's crumbling empire.

There was still one man to be caught – the Italian version of Lord Haw Haw, the traitorous English voice of Rome Radio: John Amery was brother of Julian and son of Leopold Amery, Cabinet Minister and then Secretary of State for India. On the enemy airwaves he had a more significant role than the odious George and Sally.

I went to Milan Radio and told them to broadcast an announcement demanding Amery's whereabouts. Someone instantly called-in to say he was being held by partisans in a City jail. I drove over with Sgt Huggett and told the Governor to produce him.

'Thank God you're here,' said a very pale Amery when led into the Governor's office with his girlfriend, an appealing French brunette in a black trouser suit. 'I thought they were going to shoot me.' His relief was premature. He was, like the hated William Joyce, a candidate for judicial murder.

Amery, small, dark and unshaven, was still wearing the black shirt which proclaimed his political sympathies. 'I've never been anti-British' he told me. 'You can read the scripts of my broadcasts through the years and you'll never find anything against Britain. I've just been very anti-communist and if at the moment I'm proved wrong, well one of these days you'll find out that I was right . . .'

I took him from his partisan jailers, to his great relief, and handed him over to our Military Police. He was later repatriated to Britain and at the Old Bailey stood trial for Treason. To save his family further humiliation Amery pleaded Guilty, was convicted and hanged. It was not a verdict of which the British judiciary could be proud.

Amery, scoundrel of a famous political family, had from childhood lacked any sense of right and wrong, but instead showed a certain style and considerable courage. At the foot of the scaffold he greeted his famous hangman Albert Pierrepoint: 'I've always wanted to meet you' he said, 'though not, of course, under these circumstances . . .'

I HAVE COME TO RESCUE YOU . . .

While I was resisting temptation among the German SS, the Italian end of Hitler's Axis had been frantically planning to pack up its gold and escape, somewhere. Mussolini, who had ruled Italy for 23 years, was living in the Villa Feltrinelli at Gargnano on Lake Garda, a few miles north of the seat of his Republican Government at Salò. He was 'protected' by a squad of German SS whose officers had orders not to let him out of their sight. This was partially because Hitler retained a sort of exasperated concern for Il Duce, who as the then dominant end of the Axis had brokered the Munich Agreement in 1938, at the start of the Führer's territorial demands. After his recent dismissal by King Emmanuel and subsequent rescue from hotel-arrest by Hitler's Colonel Skorzeny, Mussolini had been relegated to a mere supplicant dependent upon the German Dictator for his safety, even in his own country.

In the beautiful lakeside villa Mussolini feared he might be seen as a prisoner – which he was, almost. Aware of his declining stature, he had become more of an eccentric philosopher than an iron-willed Dictator. He was of course distressed by the destruction of his homeland as foreign nations fought through it, and by the sight of roving gangs of armed partisans – ranging from sturdy fighters to sanctioned looters – who were taking over the streets from his Blackshirts.

In December '44 Mussolini had visited Milan with General Karl Wolff, Commander of the SS in Italy, and the German Ambassador Rudolf Rahn. To their surprise, the Milanese went wild with enthusiasm, an excited crowd of 40,000 chanting *Duce! Duce! Duce!* as in the old days. Mussolini later told his wife Donna Rachele, 'It was like a tidal wave.' At Feltrinelli he had been lethargic, morose and pessimistic, but the unexpected cheers of his countrymen were invigorating and gave him confidence to attempt a stronger line with his protectors.

Unknown to Mussolini, General Wolff had been negotiating with the Allies for the surrender of the German armies in Italy with the Archbishop of Milan, Cardinal Idelfonso Schuster as intermediary. The Cardinal was also urging the Germans to come to terms with the partisans, who were growing more numerous as the war neared its end and the Allies supplied more arms. On March 8 General Wolff travelled to Berne in Switzerland to talk with Alan Dulles, Head of the OSS, the American Intelligence Service. Ten days later he met Lieutenant General Terence Airey, Chief of Staff at AFHQ, on the frontier at Ascona, Lake Maggiore, to discuss terms of surrender.

On returning to his headquarters, General Wolff received an ominous telephone message from his Commander in Berlin, SS Chief Heinrich Himmler. It warned him that his family had been taken under the personal supervision of the Gestapo, and forbade him to leave Italy again. Then on February 18 came the summons to Berlin. For German Generals whom the Nazi hierarchy believed had stepped out of line, such an order could prove fatal – as it had for General Rommel. The redheaded grey-eyed Wolff made his will, said goodbye to his friends, and flew to Berlin.

Above: Christmas dinner was celebrated traditionally in the Villa. AFPU's other ranks were waited on by the Commanding Officer, Major the Lord Stopford, Lieut. Craig, me, and Lieut. Groom.

Left: Our cookhouse did its best with army rations . . .

Below: . . . and in the end, we were all looked after rather well!

Above: Jeeps are superb vehicles – but no one ever accused them of being comfortable. Driver Talbot and I enjoyed them in the summer . . .

Below: . . . but come winter, the object of the exercise was to find wheels that were a bit cosier.

Above: As we moved north after the Germans, the Apennines grew cold.

Below: It became apparent that Italy in the winter was *no* place for a convertible.

Right: So I came down from the mountains and commandeered an unmilitary Fiat Coupé . . .

Below: This saw me through the rest of the war in comfort.

Left: Sixty years later, when I returned to Italy to shoot *Whicker's War,* I used the current Jeep production model, little changed after 60 years. It still had a lot of engine, without embarrassing you by too much comfort.

Above: Having come to terms with the SS, I went on to Radio Milan and told them to broadcast a demand for the whereabouts of John Amery, the Italian 'Lord Haw Haw' who spoke for the Fascist regime from Radio Rome. Within minutes we learned he was in a city jail.

Above: Led into the Governor's office with his French girlfriend, Amery was still wearing the black shirt that proclaimed his Fascist sympathies. Later, accused of Treason at the Old Bailey, he pleaded guilty to save his family further humiliation, was convicted, and hanged.

Left: Benito Mussolini – Il Duce – ruled Italy for 23 years. The day before Hitler and Eva Braun committed suicide in their Berlin bunker, Mussolini and his mistress Clara Petacci were shot by Italian Communists.

Right: They and fifteen Fascist Ministers, friends and employees were killed without mercy, then hung like sides of beef outside a garage in Milan's Piazzale Loreto.

A stroll to the *Gazzettino* office each morning along Venice's Riva Schiavoni; beats the Underground, any day.

Left: Venice, with a personal launch, was the perfect peacetime posting and positive compensation for those bad wartime moments.

Above: Then, for a break from the pressure of life in Venice, a short drive north to the blushing Dolomites and our Sound of Music shot. It's bad enough in black and white – you should see it in colour!

Left: The SS Headquarters in Milan was in a bank building, now the Bank of China, and guarded by all their threatening machine guns. The threat hanging over this place today is equally smart, if not quite as fatal: traffic wardens.

Above: Dawn at Pachino – the scene of the war's first assault landing . . .

Right: Peter Beach at Anzio. The invasion that started so well – but took five months to finish.

Below: There was a price to pay. A British Commonwealth cemetery at Catania, in Sicily.

Hitler was already in his bunker and Himmler became unsure how to use his effective General. After a meeting with a dazed and confused Hitler, Wolff was finally sent back to Italy with permission to meet Allied representatives on the Swiss frontier, once again. There Wolff agreed final details of an unconditional surrender. At Cardinal Schuster's palace in Milan he met representatives of the partisans who confirmed their expectation of the same terms, and told him they had given orders for a nation-wide insurrection on April 25.

Mussolini knew nothing of all this, though since March had accepted that victory was impossible. His son Vittorio, known to be unintelligent, was sent to mediate with Cardinal Schuster about the possibility of peace discussions with the Allies. The Germans were not informed.

Abbot Pancini, one of the Duce's trusted friends, visited the Papal Nuncio in Berne, Monsignor Bernardini, to explain that Mussolini knew Himmler wanted to treat with the Allies, but Hitler did not. He also told the Monsignor that the 61-year-old Mussolini had become 'very unstable', contradicting himself on policy matters within minutes.

As the only reply to his eleventh-hour peace proposals was still 'Unconditional Surrender', Mussolini fell back on his plan for a last redoubt around Sondrio in the alpine Valtellina, close to the Swiss border. He continued to believe that once the war with Germany was over the Allies would move their armies north from Italy to block the Russian advance into central Europe.

As the German front in the Po Valley began to crumble, Mussolini finally decided to defy the Germans and move himself and some of his Government to the Prefecture at Palazzo Monforte in Milan. He was convinced that if the city fell he could escape along Lake Como, protected by retreating German divisions, and join the Fascists' last stand at Sondrio.

The Swiss representative to Salò had told him that his Government would grant asylum to the families of leading Fascists. He and his Ministers would be admitted, but then interned. Mussolini was much relieved. Later the Swiss Government changed its mind.

Mussolini assured his wife Donna Rachele that the Swiss had agreed to receive her, so she should seek asylum with their younger children. He gave her various carefully guarded papers, including letters from Winston Churchill which he believed would get her across the border. His final advice was: 'Ask to be handed over to the English.' In fact, she was turned back at the frontier.

Italian aircraft he could use were still standing on the Ghedi airfield south of Brescia, and only 50 miles away. His Ministers advised him to escape to Switzerland, or Spain. Chief of Police Tamburini proposed a flight to Polynesia. Mussolini rejected the ideas with some anger. He also dismissed a melodramatic plan by his mistress, Signorina Claretta Petacci, that she stage a car accident after which it could be announced he had been killed. Following Wolff's betrayal, the apologetic Germans gave him a legitimate chance of escape to Switzerland, with honour. This he also refused: 'I'm going to meet my fate in Italy.' Then he prepared to leave for Como, reassuringly close to the Swiss border.

In a meeting with Cardinal Schuster on April 25 attended by three representatives of the partisan force, the Committee of National Liberation, the Cardinal finally admitted to Mussolini that the Germans had, through him, been negotiating for peace. This produced an Italian explosion, with Mussolini shouting 'Now I can say Germany has stabbed Italy in the back! The Germans have always treated us as slaves. Now I am free to act as I like.'

He ordered immediate departure for Como with his

entourage, telling the German officer in charge of his escort, 'Your General Wolff has betrayed me.'

He was wearing the uniform of the Fascist Militia and carrying a machine gun and two leather bags full of documents.

This was the crucial moment in Mussolini's life and death. Had he then decided to control his anger and surrender he could have waited safely in the Archbishop's palace until American or British troops arrived. There would have been no bloodshed in Milan and later he would have held the stage dramatically at his War Crimes trial. Now he had only three days to live.

He had often foreseen his death, and in an interview with an Italian journalist prophesied, 'After the struggle is over they will spit on me – but later, perhaps, they will come to wipe me clean.' He said goodbye to a friendly priest, speaking like a dying man making his final confession: 'I know I shall be shot. Who knows where we shall die, and where our bones will be thrown?'

Mussolini's melancholy had taken over much of his life. He now answered the angry tantrums of his wife and the frequent tears of his mistress by turning his back and walking away, stony-faced. At 33 the attractive Clara was 28 years his junior. They had been together for eight years, after she had written him fan letters as a star-struck schoolgirl. They first met when she called 'Duce! Duce!' at his Alfa Romeo as he passed her cycling group of youngsters on their way home from Ostia beach. Mussolini, never one to let a pretty girl pass by, stopped his car and started a relationship which led to her permanent suite in the Palazzo Venezia.

That evening as the tragedy progressed he left the security of the Archbishop's palace for Como with a small loyal group in a final furious gesture of independence. He ordered Alessandro Pavolini, his Minister of Popular Culture who now commanded the Black Brigades, to transfer them all to Sondrio. Otherwise he had no coherent plan of action. They headed north in a convoy of 30 cars and trucks, including an Alfa Romeo with diplomatic plates driven by Clara's brother Dr Marcello Petacci, who told people he was the Spanish Ambassador. They were followed by two lorries of SS, and arrived before midnight to hear that the local Blackshirts had signed a surrender with the partisans.

With an additional escort of Republican soldiers and two armoured cars they drove north through the night to Menaggio, ten miles from Switzerland. Mussolini still carried his machine gun and, though his Fascist military were deserting fast, still believed that a strong force of do-or-die Blackshirts awaited him at Sondrio. This was less than an hour's drive away through high mountains on the scenic road east towards Bolzano and the Dolomites.

Alessandro Pavolini had assured Mussolini he would bring 3,000 of his Blackshirts for an historic last-stand in the Valtellina. Such an ending amid alpine beauty, doubtless with thunder and lightning effects, appealed to Mussolini's sense of drama. Then Pavolini, who had arrived in an armoured car, finally admitted he had only *twelve* men. The other 2,988 had gone home.

That was the moment when hope died, when the Duce gave up. He realised there was no will to fight left in the Italian Socialist Republic. Weary and now apathetic, he allowed the German Lieutenant in charge of his escort to arrange for him and his few remaining followers to join a German convoy of 200 men retreating north along the lakeside, hoping to reach the Stelvio Pass and Innsbruck, in Austria.

At seven in the morning at Musso, of all places, at the north end of Lake Como and only about seventeen miles from Switzerland and safety, the convoy was fired on from the cover of a partisan roadblock – a massive tree trunk and boulders.

David Barbieri, a Captain in the 52nd Garibaldi Brigade, told the German officers escorting Mussolini's convoy that to save bloodshed he would allow their soldiers to pass, but his men had orders to arrest any Fascists.

During an afternoon of bargaining and confusion Mussolini waited in an armoured car with Clara sitting on its roof, silently weeping. Then he was persuaded to put on a German Corporal's greatcoat and helmet and hide in the back of the last truck.

The convoy drove a couple of miles north to Dongo, where partisans waited. They had been warned that Mussolini was in one of the trucks by a passing cyclist who had spotted the famous features. At the back of the third lorry they confronted an elderly man wearing a steel helmet over his bandaged head and an army overcoat. He had a machine gun across his knees.

The exhausted Mussolini made no attempt to use the gun, and told his German escort not to risk their lives trying to save him. There seemed little question of that. As the war lurched towards its climax, his escort had grown weary of dashing about guarding a moody foreign Dictator and his excitable Ministers; now they just wanted to go home, like the rest of their defeated Army. So the convoy continued its journey north to safety, but without the Duce and Clara, and the partisans contacted their HQ to ask what they should do with such famous prisoners. Their Commander at Dongo, Count Pierluigi Bellini was finally told to bring them back to Milan or, if he feared a rescue attempt, to find a safe hiding place in the mountains.

After a meal, Mussolini cheered-up and discussed the world situation with his young guards; Stalin was one of the greatest men living, he said, and Russia would be the war's only victor. The British Empire would collapse. Towards midnight he went to bed.

Next day, he and Clara were taken to a hideaway, a mountain

farm and safe house near Bonzanigo, home of Giacomo and Lia de Maria who in the past had sheltered partisans on the run from Fascists.

Mussolini, soaked by a rainstorm, refused food and sat gazing silently out of the window. He did not attempt to acknowledge or reply to the love and fatal loyalty he had inspired. Clara accepted a cup of coffee-substitute from Maria, who then turned her two sons out of their double bed and sent them into the loft. She prepared the bedroom for her guests.

Clara shyly asked for a second pillow for Mussolini. When one was found she saw there was a darn in the pillowcase so quietly put it on her side of the bed and gave Mussolini hers – a tiny but telling gesture of everyday love. (Later, when it was all over and Signora de Maria went back to her house-cleaning and washing, she found the darned pillowcase was covered with tearstains amid the mascara. That was all that remained from the alpine tragedy).

During the night two young partisans sat on guard at the bedroom door listening to murmured conversation. Outside there was the thunder and lightning of an alpine storm, but Mussolini slept.

In Milan next day, seven men of the Committee of National Liberation decided that Walter Audisio should collect Mussolini and Clara and bring them back to Milan. Audisio was a tall pallid 36-year-old bookkeeper and former anti-Fascist volunteer in Spain who called himself 'Colonel Valerio'. Believing the meeting was over, some members left. The hard-core communists then sat-on, and agreed that Mussolini and Clara should indeed be brought back . . . but *dead*.

A general demand for execution had earlier been issued by the head of the Italian Communist Party, Palmiro Togliatti. It decreed that Mussolini and his Ministers should be shot as soon as captured and identified. That decision was not revealed to non-communist members of the Committee, who felt honour-bound by the terms of the armistice to hand Mussolini over to the Allies. In order to avoid a summary execution, three attempts had already been made to find and arrest him, two by Americans and one by the Italian government in the south. All failed.

Audisio, the executioner, unconcerned by honour or armistice agreements, left Milan in a small car at 7 o'clock next morning with Aldo Lampredi, a workman who also called himself Colonel. Twelve partisans were in a following van. At Como they found the local group had already prepared cells in the town jail for their valuable prisoners and were reluctant to hand them over to two unknown 'Colonels' from Milan. After a lot of shouting and authority flashing, it was finally agreed that Mussolini and Petacci could be taken, provided Audisio signed a receipt for them. That was not too difficult.

Before he left the room Audisio stopped acting and angrily announced his real intention: 'I've come to shoot Mussolini.'

With that he drove up to the de Marias' alpine farmhouse and, with a gun in his hand, told the two prisoners, 'I have come to rescue you.' Mussolini could see what *that* meant, and was scornful; but it was as though he had already accepted final defeat. After his disastrous declaration of war in 1940, less than five years before, everything had gone wrong. Now only his death would settle his growing debt to the Italian people. The Duce's almost-successful dream of glory was ending the day before Hitler and Eva Braun committed suicide.

Mussolini and Clara were taken down to the Villa Belmonte, a large village house behind a stone wall. As soon as they got out of the car in the courtyard Clara, sensing what was about to happen, tried to protect her podgy lover, flinging her arms around him and shouting back at Audisio, 'No – you mustn't do it, you *mustn't.'* She was hysterical, Audisio damp with sweat; only Mussolini showed little emotion.

Twice Audisio tried to shoot, but each time the machine gun jammed. Before the third attempt the valiant Clara rushed at him and grabbed the barrel of his gun. He knocked her aside and pulled out a pistol – which also would not fire. He shouted for his driver's French machine gun. Mussolini faced him holding back the lapels of his jacket. 'Shoot me in the chest' he said, calmly.

They were his last words.

Another shot killed the loyal and loving Clara, who fell to the ground without a sound. Mussolini, not quite dead, groaned. Audisio shot the body once again, into the chest. Then they drove away, to kill elsewhere. It was twenty minutes past four on April 28, 1945.

In the closing days of resistance fighting, the Germans had demanded that a fraught Mussolini sanction various atrocities, including the execution of ten Italians for every German soldier killed by a partisan. He had permitted Fascist groups to do much as they wished, and agreed that Italian troops fighting with the Allies could be shot as they surrendered. His death would now reflect those brutal decisions.

In Dongo, Audisio supervised the machine-gunning of 15 of the Duce's final followers, who paid with their lives for their last-minute indecision – or loyalty. They included three Ministers, Clara's brother Marcello Petacci, Mussolini's young secretary Luigi Gatti, and Pietro Lacistri – whose only crime was that he was the Duce's personal pilot. Their bodies were thrown into the van. Clara and Mussolini were later chucked in on top of them.

Like a hired hit man, Audisio, pale and bloodless killer of seventeen unarmed countrymen, had eagerly completed his task. By that evening he had shot his name into a cruel historical footnote. Perhaps back in Milan that night after his day of pitiless barbarity he would sleep well. Perhaps not.

The German armies in Italy signed an unconditional surrender next day, while the bodies were being driven to Milan as trophies. It was a Sunday. In the early morning of April 29 the removal van acting as a hearse passed through several American roadblocks on its way to the garage in Piazzale Loreto, where nine months earlier 15 partisans had been executed by Blackshirts. Now the corpses were tipped out on to the road, to be hung-up by the ankles on the garage forecourt.

Two young men came up and kicked Mussolini repeatedly in the face. Bleeding, gashed and bullet-ridden, his body was surrounded by jeering, spitting Italians – some of whom had doubtless been among the crowds cheering him a week earlier. Those with pistols shot at his body. As the mob screamed and hit-out at the lifeless faces, one woman fired five shots into the corpse, to avenge five dead sons.

News of the savagery in the Piazzale Loreto reached us as we were filming the surrender and departure of the SS. We rushed through Milan to record the end of hopeless Fascist dreams, wondering what the dying war still had to offer in drama and surprise . . .

It had quite enough. Bloodlust unsated and in a vicious and merciless mood, an hysterical mob had subjected the corpses to sickening indignities. Mussolini's face was now appallingly disfigured. The baying mass, now brutish, demanded to see each body, calling out name after name. One after the other, the bodies were lifted for inspection.

Mussolini was held up first, to the loudest screams. Then the carcasses were strung up, and the butchery was on display.

It was not a noble way to end a war.

Not until the body of Clara Petacci was hung upside down in

the morning light next to her lover did the crowd quieten, the jeering and screaming die away. It was as though at the sight of beauty defiled, the mob suddenly realised they had murdered an attractive Italian woman who was innocent of any crime, and killed without trial the Duce they had revered and followed for almost a quarter of a century.

It is charitable to believe that Claretta's countrymen would not have wished her to die in that way alongside the fallen Dictator, but given the temper of the time and the vicious mob hysteria she may well have been spared an even worse fate.

Churchill was distressed by her 'treacherous and cowardly' murder. He had seen a photograph of the final scene and was profoundly shocked. He took time to send a telegram to Field Marshal Alexander demanding, 'Was she on the list of war criminals? Had he any authority from anybody to shoot this woman? It seems to me the cleansing hand of British military power should make inquiries on these points.'

The stolen gold of Dongo was never found, despite 'inquiries'. The grubby hands of partisan military power had faced my two choices – and made the *other* one.

THE CALL-BACK SEEMED WORSE THAN THE CALL-UP . . .

The war was over and the world had been spared an Italian Nuremberg. Field Marshal Kesselring, who had made our armies pay dearly for every yard of Italy recaptured, did make some effort to save its heritage of ancient monuments, but had not spared the lives of any of the 335 Italian hostages in the Ardeatine Cave executions. In March '44 a partisans' bomb hidden in a rubbish bin in Rome's Via Rasella had killed 32 marching SS men, and wounded many others. The bombers escaped. After a three month trial before a British court martial in May '47, 'Smiling Albert' was condemned to death for war crimes which included ordering the execution of civilians in reprisal for partisan activities.

Both Churchill and Field Marshal Alexander thought the sentence too harsh and urged that it be commuted. In a cable to the new Prime Minister, Clement Attlee, Alexander declared, 'As his old opponent on the battlefield, I have no complaint against him. Kesselring and his soldiers fought hard but clean.' Others disagreed, citing in particular his authorisation of the deportation of Italian Jews, and the stern sentences for partisans.

I attended the earlier trials of General Mältzer, Commandant of Rome, and General von Mackensen, Commander of the Fourteenth Army, in Rome in November '46. Both were found guilty of complicity in the massacre, and sentenced to be shot. This was commuted to life imprisonment, after it was contended that the military court had failed to recognise that the SS could act independently and not as part of the military chain of command. Mältzer died in prison, von Mackensen was released after five years, in 1952, and died in 1969.

So much anti-German feeling was demonstrated by the Romans at the first trial that to avoid a riot Kesselring's trial was moved to Venice. His death sentence was also reduced to life imprisonment by the Reviewing Authority, General Sir John Harding – Alexander's former Chief of Staff.

After five years of declining health but growing popularity in Germany, Kesselring was also released in 1952 as an act of clemency. He died eight years later, aged 74.

From 1945, all ranks of the victorious Eighth were being sent home to be demobbed. I had been late in to the Army – so would be late out. By then the Film Unit was fading away, so I moved from Rome to Venice to take over the Forces newspaper *Union Jack* from Hugh Cudlipp and William (Cassandra) Connor. Venice must be the world's prize posting, and as Editor I had a grand office in the Venetian daily *Il Gazzettino* and not too much work – which seemed about right.

Living in peaceful Venice was like belonging to an exclusive club. The Piazza San Marco had reverted to its role as a stately medieval drawing room where members socialised over negronis at Florian and Quadri, or bellinis round the corner at Harry's, nodding to friends as Venetian life drifted elegantly around the tables.

I never lost my joy and wonder at the Sea City, and never have; Venice grasps you, and never lets you go. Each time I pass down the Grand Canal in a vaporetto or a stylish launch, it is as though I'm seeing all that beauty for the first time. I doubt whether she has ever been as lovely or as happy as in that spring of '46, when we were all enchanted just to be alive . . .

I was quite ready to become a permanent Venetian, despite the sorry fact that my chief sub-editor, a very competent company sergeant major, had been demobilised and I had to combine his role with mine. This cruel blow meant working very hard indeed. Even so, the fête continued.

My local was Harry's Bar, created by Cipriani and in those days less well known than it became when featured in an Ernest Hemingway novel, and smart international travellers began to appreciate its simple elegance. I even opened my first account there, which meant I could saunter out through its swing doors without a vulgar exchange of cash. I felt most sophisticated. What it really meant was that all those small daily financial shocks were combined into one stunning monthly blow – when I really missed the SS trunk which had briefly been mine, all mine . . .

Life was so good in Venice that I felt I should throw a gold ring into the sea – until a Correspondent friend who had become Editor of *Exchange Telegraph* broke the spell by telling me it was about time I returned to reality. The call-back seemed worse than the call-up.

Reluctantly I left my Venetian friends in their palaces within that stunning self-obsessed cul-de-sac and caught a slow train away from the Sweetest Life back to cold rationed Austerity London.

They sent my medals through the post – a small box containing concentrated apprehension. I gave my demob suit away, and that was that. To the Victor, the demob suit.

Yet on reflection the Army had not just been a squandering of youthful years. I had already seen the best and the worst of life. I could now take photographs and write clearly, at least. Despite itself, the Army had given me a useful shove towards *Whicker's World*. It had been at once tedious and exciting, fearful and inspiring, misery and joy. It had shown me something of the world, and how people behaved under pressure. I'd seen courage and weakness, and a lot of violence. I knew how to appreciate good luck and fellowship, how to have a good time and suffer a bad time, how to relish happiness when it came my way, and be content.

So at the end of Whicker's War I put my uniform away and prepared for the demands of civilian life, braced by the judgment of Dr Johnson: 'Every man thinks meanly of himself' he said 'for *not* having been a soldier.'

WHATEVER HAPPENED TO TIME MARCHING ON . . . ?

Never go back, they say. Nasty shocks await. Memory is kind, reality is not. All this is true – but then Channel 4 asked me to rewind 60 years and return to Sicily and my old Eighth Army battlefields. I decided on reflection that I would probably be immune from further punishment since I'd suffered enough unpleasantness, the first time around. Dues had been paid – surely?

I also assumed few memories – good or bad – would survive more than half a century of development. Villas and foxholes would all now be rubble beneath hypermarkets, blood-drenched wadis softened and overgrown by innocent wild flowers, beaches washed clean of horror, woods we fought through reclaimed by lovers and nightingales. It may not be easy to ruin hundreds of miles of coastline, but the determined urban growth of Italy in the past half-century surely meant that nothing identifiable would remain? Six-lane autostrade flung across the landscape must flatten any nostalgia.

Having convinced myself that such an unwise and distressing pilgrimage would merely disturb sleeping memories and old ghosts – not to mention me – I of course *instantly* packed and flew eagerly to Catania to search for the beach where it began, and the mountains where it ended.

Sicily, which has only been part of Italy since 1860, has been invaded, conquered and settled by many peoples during 3,000 years. My Eighth and Fifth Armies were merely the last to be absorbed, our two-year passage paid for with blood and tears – and then dismissed from the memory with a shrug and a merry wave. What did you expect?

This was where war could still be chivalrous, as in the Western Desert: a clean contest between warriors, with mutual respect. A *gentlemanly* battle, without rancour. Certainly the Italians, blending tragedy with farce, could never take any war seriously.

En route for Sicily we had one stop, at Florence – most happily anticipated. Our 146 came over the runway to land and I was already spotting noble locations when the engine note changed and we were back on full power, climbing urgently through the everyday housing surrounding the airport, as though on second thoughts we had just remembered a more important engagement.

The Captain had decided the crosswinds were too strong. He turned north and flew above the route the Fifth Army had taken in '44, up through the Futa Pass and the Gothic Line. We landed on the longer runway of our old target, Bologna, after 30 painless minutes instead of six painful months.

Next morning, south to Sicily and Pachino beach, where Mediterranean life and death began. Return visits awakening old memories rarely fit into planned programmes of reminiscence. Instant nostalgia gets brushed aside by an horizon full of high-rises. The world cannot wait for memories to catch up. Yes, OK, understood – but this time my old battlefront sanctuaries of 60 years ago were . . . *unchanged*.

Is this possible in days when, if you turn your back, new towns and housing estates arrive and the horizon is transformed? When few vistas survive? Whatever happened to relentless Time Marching On?

I had expected every wartime refuge would be long gone, yet right up the boot of Italy they still stood just as I recalled. I kept reliving old dreams and nightmares, dancing about with delight, or standing stunned by distant sorrow. Yes, but my old comrades, friends, enemies – where are *they*?

Gone. All of them gone. Not one left to hear of my discoveries, happy or sad. So always make the most of people you will miss, while you have the chance.

I drove first to the beach where I waded ashore on that return to Europe. Pachino village had grown and a few buildings were scattered along the coast road; but the sea was as gentle, the sand soft and sympathetic and still ready to embrace and sustain a flinching body diving for cover. Sicily had healed – though on my return it was scorched and breathless after a brutal 40° African summer. Was Europe really as parched as this, the first time around – or was I too busy to notice?

Now it was dawn, so the beach was deserted, the sea calm and still – until a great orange ball climbed out of the Mediterranean horizon and up in to the sky. This was where we waded ashore, wondering whether that half-buried *thing* was a mine . . . whether the next step would bring an explosion. Now nothing was moving, except memories.

Sicily, traditionally the poorest and emptiest part of Italy, is about to become fashionable – the new Tuscany – and as a Sicilian ruin can be half the price of a Tuscan ruin, an uneven prosperity is promised. Seduced by this golden edge of Europe, developers are arriving to discover that Mafiosi usually keep to themselves in their own villages (good) and that whatever you buy has two prices: one for Sicilians, the other for you (bad).

Driving inland we spotted a stylish farmhouse converted into an attractive but basic hotel, and moved in. Vivid bougainvillea lined the sandstone, and no one bothered to pick up fallen lemons.

We drove on to my first discovery of the war – we could have called it, a capture. The ancient city of Noto, once capital of the region and still, as a UNESCO World Heritage site, protected from much unsympathetic central development. The surroundings are standard-dreadful.

Destroyed by an earthquake in 1693, it was rebuilt into the finest baroque town in Sicily. Great golden buildings cluster around the 17th century Cathedral, alleyways are full of flash cars, butchers' shops and ice cream cafés where locals eat granita for breakfast and dark-eyed dark-tanned girls dip their rolls into icy sorbets.

Along lanes in the arid countryside around town, the well-built pillboxes I filmed in '43 were still there, still unused. Ugly rectangular blocks of Russian-style flats now stand above ruined farm cottages and derelict overgrown huts soon to be converted, no doubt, into somebody's Des Res. Sicily is beautiful, but brutal – an island of dusty cacti and sandy wasteland, impatient with half measures.

Normally only victorious nations celebrate wars and conflicts; in defeated Sicily, soft-spoken historians lead the public through splendid little war museums full of expensive special-effects displays as seen in the Imperial War Museum, but rarely elsewhere. I even saw some of my own photographs, far better presented than at home.

In a world of trash television and so-called clean wars where precision-bombing can limit casualties and occasional communiqués keeping score sorrowfully record '3 deaths', it seemed strange to wish to keep alive details of bloody battles within memory where deaths were counted in hundreds or thousands, and casualties in scores of thousands – and where the national role was confused and often inglorious.

We revisited two British war cemeteries, which always tug at your heart in that direct and inescapable way. Amid thousands of white crosses crisply at attention a lone gardener was mowing soft grass in the cruel mid-day heat, and caring for his agapanthus and roses. As always, the whole place was impeccable. Some graves had sad little inscriptions from devastated parents. Others, unnamed, were even sadder: 'Known only to God'.

A Jewish member of our camera crew said quietly, 'Without these people, we wouldn't be alive.' We stood and looked at the careful symmetry of crosses and a few stars stretching into the distance across this foreign field, at the final resting places of our defenders and champions – many of them 18 or 19 – and knew that it was true. The graveyard bordered an autostrada and the city's airport, yet seemed peaceful and serene.

Rest In Peace, quiet young heroes come to die in Sicily.

Leaving such tranquillity and heading north, we passed through Lentini on the malarial plain outside Catania – which surprisingly the Eighth Army selected as its headquarters site when held up by determined Panzer Grenadiers around Etna. These days it is not so much the mosquitoes that keep people away as the fact that it is home to Mafia families.

It seemed no more menacing than other small places in Sicily. As a wandering television man I always feel professionally neutral when liable to be threatened. I remember filming an early *Whicker's World* about Sardinian bandits, who can also be unwelcoming. I emerged undamaged, protected by my innocent belief in neutrality and my determination to smile at everybody, especially if armed. Since I've hardly ever been shot I must be doing something right.

Sardinian bandits at Nuoro, Mafia from Palermo, Camorra in Naples can all complicate filming. I have had no dealings with the Camorra, I'm happy to say, though earlier on this shoot was accepted by lines of Neapolitan motorists as a local Capo. I'm not sure if this was flattering but it *was* effective. We were driving to Castellammare from where the Anzio fleet had sailed and needed pictures with Mount Vesuvius magnificent in the background. We parked our cars and, to keep the foreground clear for the shot, had briefly to hold up traffic while I stood in the road waiting to do a piece to-camera. Our interpreter prepared to go from car to car apologising and explaining.

The reaction was dramatic. Drivers in the first cars instantly closed their windows, locked the doors and stared straight ahead. They never heard her – yet she was an attractive girl. Whatever it was would be bad news. Several cars further back in the queue did frantic u-ies in the road and hurtled away. Some backed-off into the distance, at speed. They all thought we were another Camorra roadblock – a kidnapping, perhaps, or maybe just a collection to replenish funds. Whatever it was, whoever I was – they wanted out.

I did my piece fast, because panic was growing. Old ladies were getting the vapours and some hothead was doubtless about to risk his life taking a pot shot at me, to claim a reward from someone.

When we waved-on the cars, they passed-by slowly, relieved and respectful. We don't see that kind of discipline at home.

On my return to the island, I drove carefully up to the holiday town of Taormina, said to be the safest place in Sicily because it is where Mafiosi send their families for the summer. Well, that's reasonable. It has a splendid position across a mountainside below Mount Etna, and spreads its sandstone ledges down towards the sea.

Delightfully pretty in a fairytale way, Taormina perches between bay and volcano on its rocky hillside, with cobbled walking streets and alleyways – but it is surprisingly unchic. Its setting could be compared with Portofino, Capri or Positano, but it has grown more package tour than *dolce vita*. Being a mite short on style may be one reason why no one has given our charming Casa Cuseni the kiss of life.

That well-proportioned villa was also *exactly* as we had left it – one of the few homes that had not been rearranged at all in 60 years. Shabby-chic, but unchanged. A little less loved perhaps, a little more overgrown – but not a brick or a tile had been renewed. Even the furniture seemed the same – and it was tired enough when we got there in '43!

It now wears that faded washed-out look fashion magazines appreciate and film companies remembering the British Raj attempt to recreate. In bright sunlight, a mite dilapidated and sad. In shadow, a mellow and elegant time capsule. Upstairs, only abandoned mattresses and forgotten lives.

It is still owned by the same family as in the Forties when requisitioned by Field Marshal Kesselring, and afterwards by Captain Whicker (less well titled, but at least *winning*). Today two concerned but elderly guardians look after it. The owner, Daphne Phelps, had written a book about 'A House In Sicily' which she nurtured for fifty years. Not too many villas are so honoured.

During the war we at least had a few weeks to relish its tranquillity, before I was called to board a waiting Landing Craft Infantry once more to go and invade somewhere and get shot at. This time, having rediscovered Casa Cuseni still there and little changed, the Insight Television shooting schedule snatched us away after a few days and we headed towards Anzio, the worst place of all, with bad dreams of horror and mutilation, and haunting echoes of dying soldiers crying for help in the darkness of no-man's-land.

Our life-saving villa above Anzio harbour was also relatively unchanged, though divided into two or three flats. The agreeable owners of the first floor, where we lived our lives, had exorcised not only shells and bombs but the careless ghost of Reynolds *(après moi le déluge)* Packard. I checked the cellar of evil memory: the rats had moved on. There were a few new and insubstantial outbuildings on its seaside but the view from the terrace was still ideal for pictures of passing shells and arriving bombs. I could not find our tripod marks.

A new block had surrounded the next door stairs down which the War Correspondents tumbled, but otherwise any retired German artilleryman looking down at us through binoculars from his OP atop the Alban Hills would have spied how delighted I was to find that his comrades had not crushed our sanctuary, nor our spirits, and that any top-hatted GI would still recognise the cellars of Nettuno which saved and restored lives. The 95th Evac Hospital was only a caring, gallant memory.

By the time we left to liberate Rome in '44 the Anzio port had already been battered beyond recognition. When our grey squadrons of landing craft sailed away, anything still standing had to come down to be rebuilt. I was happy to discover that the new harbour with its restaurants and fishermen is charming and quite unlike the concrete monoliths of neighbouring Ostia. I don't know how it escaped the infestation of modern blocks which spring up across most Italian seasides – especially since this one is only an hour's drive from the homes of millions of Romans.

It took us rather longer to reach Rome because of weekend traffic. I kept seeing the shades of Clara and her friends, cycling joyfully beside Mussolini's Alfa Romeo and crying *Duce! Duce!*, unaware of the intense happiness and sorrow to come . . .

In Rome I went straight to the Hotel de la Ville in the Via Sistina, which had housed German officers and then British Public Relations. Behind new partitions its pleasant courtyard was hidden, but I could see the terrace of my top floor bedroom still had its view of the Spanish Steps.

I drove on to Florence, my second favourite city. Even with a local friend it took a long time to reach the Villa Paradisino on the Via Belisario Vinta where I lived during that last terrible winter of war; it used to take five minutes.

Once again – I still can't believe I'm writing this after 60 years – the villa was *unchanged,* though surrounded by a tortuous system of one-way lanes. These meant you no longer crossed the Arno on the Ponte di Ferro and took the second left. Now you follow a circuitous route which heads off towards Siena and then winds back through the Piazzale Michelangelo before dropping down into another complication of lanes.

Today's owners are a handsome and agreeable couple; he a lawyer, she an elegant chatelaine who had a distant connection with the former owners, my late friends the Ludovico Daneos. The house had been extravagantly redecorated and was as desirable as ever, including the mandatory Alsatian guarding the portals.

In Milan, I found the old SS headquarters on the avenue from the Duomo to La Scala, at a right-hand junction with a minor road. The three-storey block is now, of course, a Bank – the Bank of China. The structure of the building seemed the same and the lobby, where they handed me many millions, was little changed, though it seems they don't proffer free money, these days. I stood there remembering the machine guns and barbed wire as the ghosts of defiant SS men marched by, defeated but not bitter. The Milanese were still milling around, but too vibrant to be ghosts, even when not jeering.

Then on to Venice, where of course I was not expecting change nor did I find any, praise be. Piazza San Marco was the same, give or take a few hundred thousand people. Harry's Bar, still splendidly unimposing, expensive and welcoming to old clients. When I risked telling them I had an account they went and looked me up, but returned mildly baffled.

I did not reveal it was in 1946, for it suddenly occurred to me their reaction might be, 'Ah yes, Capitano Whicker, we've been waiting for half-a-century. Risotto and scampi for two, with a bottle of prosecco? Your outstanding bill is now a trillion lire including tax, service – and interest.'

THE SAGA OF THE D-DAY DODGERS . . .

The American-born Lady Astor succeeded her Tory husband as MP for Plymouth in 1949, and so became the first woman to sit in the House of Commons. Before she died in 1964 she had many an acerbic passage-at-arms with Winston Churchill, but was never sillier than when she chose to dismiss British forces fighting the Wehrmacht in Italy as 'The D-Day Dodgers'. This unfortunate phrase suggested that the Eighth and Fifth Armies were having a cushy time away from the Second Front in France. She was evidently unaware that Allied forces in Italy had fought several D-Days of their own in savage and bloody battles, suffering fearful casualties in Great War conditions.

Weary tormented men in Italy could only neutralize their anger by treating her waspish inanity as a silly joke. The *Eighth Army News* published a number of replies, after some attention to scansion and delicacy. Some were scornful, some rueful, others bitter; all followed the tune of their desert anthem, Lili Marlene.

Its original authors long lost, 'The Dodgers' came in many versions – all doggerel, until the last verse. This is one of them:

We're the D-Day Dodgers, out in Italy
Always on the vino – always on the spree
Eighth Army scroungers with our tanks
We live in Rome among the swanks
The carefree D-Day Dodgers, out in Italy

We landed at Salerno, a holiday with pay
The Germans brought a band out, to cheer us on our way
They showed us sights and gave us tea
We all sang songs – the beer was free
To welcome D-Day Dodgers to sunny Italy

Naples and Cassino were taken in our stride
We didn't go to fight there, we just went for the ride
Anzio and Sangro were just Italian names
We really only went there to look-around for dames
The artful D-Day Dodgers, in Northern Italy

Along the way to Florence we had a lovely time
We ran a bus to Rimini, right through the Gothic Line
Soon on to Bologna we will go
And after that, we'll cross the Po
Then we'll be D-Day Dodgers, all over Italy

Once we heard a rumour we were going home
Back to dear old Blighty, never more to roam
Then someone said 'In France you'll fight'
So we said 'No, we'll just sit tight'
The windy D-Day Dodgers, still out in Italy

We hope the boys in France will soon get home on leave
With all of six months' service in, it's time for *their* relief
But we'll all carry on out here
For at least another year
Contented D-Day Dodgers, who serve in Italy

Dear Lady Astor knows a lot
Standing talking tommy rot
She may well be the nation's pride
But we all think the mouth's too wide!
Her loving D-Day Dodgers, in far off Italy

Just look around the mountains, amid the mud and rain
You'll find those scattered crosses, some without a name
Heartbreak, toil and suffering gone
The lads beneath them slumber on
They are the D-Day Dodgers, who'll *stay* in Italy . . .

ACKNOWLEDGEMENTS

As always, my thanks go first to Valerie, who retraced every step with me, from scorching beach to icy Alp – and finally, bravely, into Harry's Bar. Some of these pictures are hers, but most are my wartime shots and red-hots. Others by AFPU cameramen, through the admirable Imperial War Museum. The memory of Harry Rignold's grave is from the Sidney Brown AFPU Collection.

Trevor Dolby, making the world go round at HarperCollins, was a wise guide. Laureen Fraser typed endlessly, shepherding my words from the air to computer to page.

My thanks also to those behind the Insight Television cameras who shot our programmes for Channel 4: Producers David Hart and son Joe; Chris Smith (camera) and Rupert Ivey (sound) provided great company and fast motoring.

Then, as always, our friends along the *Whicker's World* flight-path who joined this kaleidoscope of Italian life, past and present. My gratitude to you all.

PICTURE CREDITS

The author and publisher are grateful to the Photograph Collection of the Imperial War Museum, London for permission to use the following:

Plate section one: page 2, top right, bottom; page 3, bottom; page 4, both; page 5, all.
Plate section two: page 1, top right; page 2, bottom left; page 3, both; page 4, both; page 5, both; page 6, all; page 7, all.
Plate section three: page 2, top; page 3, top right, bottom; page 4, all; page 5, top; page 6; page 7, both; page 8, middle.
Plate section four: page 1, middle.

All other photographs reproduced courtesy of the author from his private collection, and are retained under his own copyright. Photography may not be reproduced without the express permission of the author.

INDEX